The Silent E

The Environmental Crisis is a Crisis of Human Consciousness

By Carlita Shaw

This book is dedicated to every human being who devotes him/herself to building bridges to a more peaceful and sustainable planet, to every environmental defender who has lost his/her freedom or life to save a species or the environment. To alternative energy inventors, medical, scientific, or engineering pioneers who have also lost their lives, freedom or had their work sabotaged because it was for the benefit of the planet and advancing mankind.

A big heartfelt thanks to all my friends and family who have supported me through difficult times and for believing in my work. Thank you to Colette, my mother for her encouragement, infinite support and love and to Karel Herman for being amazing in every way. Thank you so much Kiara Montross for helping me beyond measure. Thank you to Kauser Khan and Julia Easty for being my longest standing friends and making me feel a part of your families. Thank you to Annelise Caron for your loving encouragement that helped keep my family together. Thank you, Teresa Durant, for being there for me and to Ken Regan for providing a space for me when I returned to Ecuador. Thank you to Carlos Andrade for being my selfless lawyer in Ecuador. Other people, I would like to thank are Trevor James Constable, Patrick Kelly, Sir John Searl, Niall Murphy, James Horack, Neil Kramer and Johana Sand for being an inspiration to me.

Thank you to all those amazing people that have given me their time to share their amazing work with the world, you have all helped make this book possible.

Endorsements

"Carlita Shaw's The Silent Ecocide is a brave call that challenges humanity to stand up and take responsibility for our future on Planet Earth.

It is a book to make each of us aware that the ecological crisis in the world today is not a simple black & white picture - it is a much broader canvas that involves our relationships to energy, economics, politics, human resources, and ultimately to our very selves.

Shaw does not hold back in pointing out our human frailties and failings; yet in the end there is hope, if we can rise to the responsibility of being conscious agents of change. As Shaw says, "Saving the world and humanity is now an inside job." I couldn't agree more.

The ecocide on planet Earth can no longer remain in silence. This book is a clear and loud voice on the planet's behalf - and we should listen."

Kingsley L. Dennis Ph.D
Author and Researcher,
www.kingsleydennis.com

"The book "The Silent Ecocide" captures incredibly the truth about human greed, which has made us exceed the planetary boundaries. The data in the book plus two decades of the writers experience in ecology is a revelation for the ultimate awakening of human consciousness. The wonders of nature are traded by the corrupt forces of market...mainly the investors....who have no right to it.

Human beings who have the smallest place in coexistence have pretended for too long to be above all. This ego has separated humanity from all forms of lives. Transformation of human consciousness becomes urgent for the survival of all forms of life and for intergenerational equity.........

Thank you and all the best for this wonderful book of yours. May human beings soon realize their follies before it is too late."

Dr. Saamdu Chetri
Executive Director
GNH Centre Bhutan
www.gnhcentrebhutan.org

GNH stands for Gross National Happiness.

About the Centre: The purpose of the Centre is to offer space from where individuals leave refreshed, invigorated, and empowered with inspiration and understanding of how to bring GNH principles, values, and practices fully and meaningfully into their daily lives and work. Going back to their own communities, they will be enthused and empowered to serve their families, neighbors, country and the world with genuine purpose, compassion and effectiveness.

"Carlita's devotion to preserving natural landscapes and indigenous cultures is unyielding. It's rare to see such loving commitment actually embodied in real life; not just in hopeful words, but in resolute actions every day. Thank heavens there are people like Carlita tackling this head on, working on the front lines, speaking the truth."

Neil Kramer,
Philosopher & Author
www.neilkramer.com

Contents

- Chapter 1: Signs of Ecocide-6
- Chapter 2: Making Money out of Hot Air-Carbon Trading-25
- Chapter 3: Oil, Politics and The Amazon Rainforest-40
- Chapter 4: We are not Protesters but Protectors-66
- Chapter 5: Ecological Economy-72
- Chapter 6: Water, Rain, Life-78
- Chapter 7: Introducing Alternative Energy-106
- Chapter 8: The Perspective of a Free Energy Inventor-134
- Chapter 9: The Ecology of Consciousness-158
- Chapter 10: Evolving to Gaia-167
- Chapter 11: The Birth of Solutions-179
- Chapter 12: Walk with Nature-194

Published by Evolve to Ecology
www.evolvetoecology.com
2nd Edition, June 2015.

Introduction

The purpose of this book is to make the reader aware of the present environmental situation around the world – where we are at now, where we are heading and what we can do to improve matters. Some of the information presented here may be unfamiliar to you, but that is only because everyone is not aware of some subjects. However, the material in this book is so important and what we choose to do in the coming years so vital, that these matters cannot be ignored or action delayed, if our future is to be a happy one.

Chapter 1: Signs of Ecocide

Many people talk about humankind witnessing an apocalypse, however, very few people realise that since the Cretaceous period, we are now living in the *Sixth* greatest mass extinction of all time. It is an apocalypse happening in slow motion which affects all of the earth's biodiversity which took 3.8 billion years of evolution to form. This extinction differs from previous extinctions in that it is caused by humans, not by natural causes, as we are the cause, we can also slow it down or prevent it, if we make big changes. Yet governments are aware of this and we continue to accelerate it, each year, and this affects every single species and ecosystem on the planet. According to recent scientific data, animals and plants are disappearing at a rate of between 75 and 150 species **per day**. There may be no rainforest left in twenty years' time or fish in the ocean in ten years' time and over half the world will have a water crisis fifteen years from now. Bees are our most important crop pollinators and are fast disappearing and the rate of deforestation and ocean pollution is destroying these keystone ecosystems, which are drastically affected by man's own actions.

As a result of the misconception that we are not deeply connected to our environment, the ecosystems of our planet show signs of devastating impact; from oceans being contaminated with almost three hundred thousand tons of floating plastic, radioactive waste, sewerage, oxygen depleted zones and over-fishing. Rainforests are rapidly disappearing; if we continue to deforest the Amazon at the current rate it may well affect the climate drastically. The science is not settled which way climatic temperatures are going, despite what the politicians want you to believe, their climate science is biased, the United Nations IPCC report on 'Global Warming' ignored 33 scientific papers out of 45. The climate has always been changing and always will change; it doesn't stay one temperature permanently. Climate change has been happening for millions of years and will continue to happen no matter what man does. This does not mean that there are no serious issues at stake environmentally, this is far from the case, we are pushing the planet to an ecologically critical tipping point, if we do not make changes now, we have very little time before it will be too late.

This is a crucial time, despite our present crisis; there is one last opportunity to make positive changes. We need to re-establish our lost connection with the Earth and the natural environment. All the current notions that man has dreamed up, create the illusion of us being separate from nature. This is, of course, completely ridiculous, as we are part of nature, we were shaped by our environment and this will never change. We have no choice in this matter nor can we afford to take a long time to understand this. It is necessary for us to accept the fact and take action individually, to lessen our human impact on Earth at our most vulnerable time. There is a slow emergence of academic literature and journals noting this crisis, a few even suggest ways in which we can re-evaluate managing our natural resources. A very recent journal article (*W. Steffen et al, 2015*), published in *The Science Journal*, entitled *Planetary Boundaries: Guiding Human Development on a Changing Planet*, states that humans have pushed the planet beyond boundaries to danger point, destabilising important ecosystems.

This not only affects biodiversity but ecosystems too, which are disregarded in human society, yet are the support systems for all life on Earth, and which need to be considered by the world economy. Ecosystems such as biogeochemical flows, are affected by industrial scale agriculture, our global fresh-water supply is dwindling and our oceans are acidifying, oxygen depleted zones are more common in the ocean now and these have a drastic effect on marine life, and as a result, algal blooms form and some areas of the ocean are now radioactive due to Japan's, Fukushima Nuclear radiation melt down disaster, which has been contaminating the Pacific ocean with a continuous outpouring of radiation, scientific readings by global civilian nuclear radiation monitoring groups have found dangerous levels of Cesium 134 and Cesium 137, Strontium and other radionuclides in seaweed and sea life along the Californian Pacific ocean, sea life in the Pacific is dying off at an alarming rate that scientists cannot measure through lack of funding and without the support and attention of governments to investigate, this really is the largest scale silent ecocide presently unfolding just in the Pacific ocean, this and the on-going effects of the Mexican Gulf Oil disaster have had a profound impact on marine life and will undoubtedly continue to have a detrimental effect on ecology and on human health, while governments conveniently ignore this silent ecocide. Aside from the ecocide that Fukushima is causing, the effects of the Gulf Oil spill killed thousands of marine animals, over a million seabirds died, 66 percent of fish species were affected, over 3,000 endangered sea turtles were affected, 1000 died immediately and 5,000 marine mammals such as whales and dolphins died as a direct result of petroleum contamination. In the month of March 2015, thousands of Sea Lions and their starved pups washed up on the coast of California, over the last four years over 4,000 Sea Lions have died this way, among those investigating the deaths, radiation is being blamed as the cause. Thousands of fish have died en-mass over the last few years in different parts of the world, and there was even a case where hundreds of Snow geese just fell out of the sky, dead birds and dead insects everywhere dying in their thousands and people are still not seeing that we are living in this slow moving Apocalypse, caused by human negligence.

The ocean is an extremely important ecosystem considering that micro-organisms in the ocean produce eighty percent of our oxygen, in comparison to the rainforest ecosystem which produces around 20 percent of oxygen. The [1]*Stefin et al* paper proposes safe management of natural resources using what these scientists call 'The Planetary Boundary Framework'. By using this system, governments could improve management of natural resources and consider the limits of these resources for the future of humanity and the planet. This is just one example of the emerging studies and technologies, which acknowledges our current crisis and are starting to state clearly that we need to start living within the means of the Earth's natural resources. However, there is very little public awareness at present of most of this material, therefore it is the goal of this book to focus on exploring solutions to the global crisis, in spite of the fact that most people continue onward with their everyday lives in the current disastrous system. At first glance, there are a number of subjects covered in this book that may seem unrelated to the reader, but they are all related to the current condition in which we find ourselves. I take each of these subjects and illustrate how they interrelate and affect the undeniable fact that the environmental crisis is a crisis of human consciousness and understanding. Our environment mirrors our state of consciousness, resulting in all of its current deformations and beauty. The increase in cancer among mankind is another indication that we need to take better care of our environment. Maintaining responsibility over our internal ecology ensures a sustainable healthy external ecology.

Capitalism has become predatory because everything in our economy is dominated by gaining money quickly, achieved at the price of destruction of the environment or a species. Our current economy operates without insight or appreciation of the long-term future of the planet or her creatures. This could all be changed if our economy embraced ecological values and sustainability of natural resources.

This reflects in the large scale environmental crisis and the accelerated rate of species extinction, a rate of extinction which is 1000 times greater than it was before humans were present on the Earth. It is estimated that around 75 to 150 entire species are disappearing every day. According to the *Red List* calculations of the IUCN (the International Union for Conservation of Nature), 22,413 of the world's species are threatened with extinction and this number is increasing as further investigations are taking place.

Almost **80 percent** of all present primates will be extinct in less than 40 years' time. For example, there are only 620 Western Silverback gorillas left in the wild. Orang-utans are native to Malaysia and Borneo, and while there are about 40,000 Orang-utans left, due to rapid destruction of their habitats with palm oil plantations and deforestation, it is likely that they will disappear within 25 years. There are fewer than 3,000 Tigers remaining in the wild. Over 36,000 Elephants were killed last year and every 15 minutes an African Elephant is killed for its Ivory. At the present rate, in ten years' time, there won't be any African Elephants or Tigers left in the wild. Extinction is now imminent for the Northern White Rhino with just one male remaining in the wild, he has armed guards surrounding him to protect him from poachers, there are only 35 Javan Rhinos left and 400 Sumatran Rhinos, so they are on the brink of extinction, and other species of Rhino have already become extinct, a few thousand Black Rhino are left in the African bush, however, the subspecies, the Western Black Rhino is now extinct, yet big game hunting is still allowed and it is now more popular than ever before.

There are about 13,000 Grey Wolves left remaining in the wild, wolves are killed systematically each year in the USA, with no acknowledgement of what they can do for the ecology of wildlife reserves, Biologists have done biodiversity surveys in Yellowstone Park, USA, where wolves have been reintroduced and discovered that when wolves are left to reproduce, they greatly enhance the biodiversity of nature, there are fewer coyotes, more songbirds, more insects, wilder elk, richer soils and their very presence increases the quality of these ecosystems, as well as adding twenty more vertebrate species that thrive from their presence, wolves are an intrinsic part of the ecosystem and when they are removed, the ecosystem suffers and biodiversity is lost. These are not subtle differences; they are vital changes when the wolf is removed from the ecology of a landscape.

There are only around 20,000 Blue Whales remaining, and only 55 of Maui dolphin species which are critically endangered, the Indus and Ganges River Dolphin, Baiji Dolphin, Hectors and Vaquati Dolphins are all endangered. Amphibians are highly sensitive bio-indicators to environmental pollution and disease, as they breathe through their skin as a secondary respiratory system and some frogs and salamanders' breath entirely through their skin, they are very vulnerable to the effects of environmental pollution on their survival, and therefore 41 percent of all amphibian species have already become extinct or are threatened with extinction. Other threatened species include 25 percent of Mammals, 13 percent of birds, 33 percent of coral reefs, and many tree and plant species.

Rainforests occupy around 5 percent of the Earth's terrestrial land, yet rainforests contain over 50 percent of the world's plants and animal species (biodiversity). There is no accounting for the number of plant and tree species fast disappearing, especially from the rainforests, which are being destroyed at a rate of 60 square kilometres **per hour**. That is the equivalent of 4,000 football pitches per hour, every hour of every day that passes, with an exponentially rising rate of biodiversity loss. Oil drilling and mining create the main impacts, cattle ranching; logging and road construction to the mines and oil extraction sites contribute to this unfolding ecocide. Forty percent of the world's logging industry is due to paper production which consumes six billion trees cut down annually to produce newspapers, magazines, toilet roll, junk mail and paper bags, if only people would take recycling more seriously, paper production is very energy costly and consumes hundreds of thousands of tons of water too, this could be avoided and greatly reduced with an increase in recycled paper products.

While the Amazon rainforest is referred to as the lungs of the planet, it is actually the world's oceans and their microbes that are the lungs of the Earth, producing 80 percent of the world's oxygen, yet the oceans are heavily polluted with plastic and toxic effluence contaminating the food chain and we continue to over-exploit over 85 percent of the world's fish stocks. Some experts say that we are the last generation to be able to fish as we do with fish stocks rapidly declining. It has also been noted by ecologists that the world's Bee populations have been decimated due to sensitivity to neonicotinoid poisons and other chemicals produced by Monsanto, Bayer and

DuPont. We need bees to pollinate our crops, most ecosystems rely on such pollinators, if bees disappear, this will speed up the rate of plant species extinction and loss of our food crops and food in general, and we cannot survive without bees!

Another possible cause of the loss of bees and other pollinators, could be due to global [2]geoengineering, which is the practice of sun obscuration using planes that spray an aerosol mixture into the atmosphere, which after twenty minutes or so spreads out over vast areas of sky, contaminants from the sprayed chemicals have been tested globally and it has been noted that aluminium nano-particles affect the bees navigation and the particles are possibly killing bees.

Dane Wigington who is an expert in Solar energy and owns a 1,600 acre wildlife reserve has noted that we have already lost twenty percent of our solar uptake due to solar obscuration caused by spraying of heavy metal particulates into the atmosphere, he began taking biological samples from plants, soils and rain water (governments admit they are doing this allegedly to cool the planet and to create a plasmic field for radio communication and HAARP waves to travel through). Dane's tests showed metallic nano-particulates such as aluminium, strontium, barium, arsenic and mercury which are being sprayed globally into the atmosphere. Environmental toxicity or human health studies have not been done by governments before launching these programmes. In the USA, tests on toxic loads in rainwater revealed 3450 parts per billion of aluminium in rain water and twenty percent of the sun's rays are now being blocked out, there has been a rise in rickets and vitamin D deficiency as a result. Our health and the health of the planet are at stake with a toxic mix of nano-particle metals and chemicals. Aluminium particles are not only toxic but they also prevent seeds from propagating, while Monsanto are creating aluminium-resistant seeds. These sun obscuration chemicals are being released in dangerous loads and are not only affecting insects, birds and fish but also possibly killing trees, forests, and are possibly to blame for the masses of dead fish and birds being documented globally, there has been a large reduction of boreal forests. Trees are dying with no explanation of what the causes are. Another aspect of this toxicity is causing respiratory problems in millions of people, the chemicals being sprayed have a synergetic toxicity when combined with mercury and other chemicals in human vaccines, it is no wonder that autism has increased with no scientific explanation other than population increase being the main factor. The ozone layer is also being decreased due to the toxins in geoengineering, not CFCs, so this in turn affects the planetary albedo; the ability to reflect the sun's rays naturally is being reduced, this has a very large effect on weather and climate change.

We are barely scratching the surface of the environmental crisis which we are in and unfortunately most environmental scientists are afraid to speak out against geoengineering, because people are accused of being *'conspiracy theorists'*, despite the growing scientific data from samples collected globally.

At the most recent [3]International Union for Conservation of Nature (IUCN) conference, in Australia in November 2014, Simon Stuart, Chair of The Species Survival Commission, stated that *"almost no country in the world is heading in the right direction considering the targets to stop species extinction by 2020"*.

Is this ecocide a reflection of short-sighted greed? Is this not a wake-up call? An opportunity to change the way we see ourselves in relation to nature? It certainly is an indication that the caring human is in danger of extinction. Governments seem either to still have their heads in the sand, or just not care at all, as if we have another planet to go to when it all comes tumbling down, we are in the middle of an apocalypse of our own doing. Or is it that politicians are just conveniently ignoring these issues because creating change would no longer mean holding power and wealth but establishing more ecological transparent governance?

We need to stop seeing ourselves as separate from our planet and our fellow creatures, what we do to our environment, we inevitably do to ourselves. Like every cell that makes up every organ in the human body, every species has a value and roll in contributing to the planet's ecosystems functioning healthily. The disappearance of so many species and the loss of rich biodiversity on such a large scale is having a detrimental effect on ecosystems worldwide already, effects we have underestimated and have little understanding of what to expect as a result of our impact on the environment.

Governments have built values around material wealth, not ecological wealth and the only way to save ourselves and the planet is by putting financial value on ecological wealth, as it is usually invisible or an abstract concept, in terms of human understanding of how much work and production goes on in nature, that we pay no attention to, let alone the way in which what we do affects the mechanisms of nature or ecosystems. Our anthropogenic impact, the effects of how we live, has deeply affected nature to a level where environmental scientists or ecologists have no time to measure our impact efficiently on each ecosystem or species that is being affected, though the signs that are appearing, point to warning signals for the future of all species on this unique planet.

The environmental crisis is a crisis of human understanding, the outer manifestation of this destruction is an indication that we need to change. We are living in a time where we need to re-establish our lost connection with the Earth.

"At a deep psychological level, convincing young people that they will get the respect, admiration, and love that they are looking for, through consumerism, is a manipulation of a deep human instinct to want to belong. Advertising and the media reinforce this message, in the process, destroying the community structures that provided people with the affirmation that they need. We have evolved in groups – deeply interdependent and connected – the separation and competition of the modern world is antithetical to our deepest needs." - Helena Norberg Hodge

[4]Helena Norberg Hodge who is an ecological pioneer and author of Ancient Futures, studied with Noam Chomsky, Founder of the Society for Ecology and Culture and believes that those running the global economy are imposing structural violence on our world.

Over the last 50 years, an ecological imbalance has arisen from the monopolisation of natural resources and energy, a monopoly that overlooks a need to create a more sustainability based economy that is within the bounds of the Earth's natural carrying capacity. Centralisation (control) of natural resources in the 'free market' causes imbalances such as socio-economic problems in the countries where these valuable natural resources are based. The result is deforestation, famine, debt, homelessness and problems for local food growers and indigenous producers, how is it justifiable that a wealthier country has helped itself to local resources leaving the natives with nothing? We need to focus on localised sustainability, basically going back to the traditional ways of farming and managing local agricultural practices. Modern industrial farming practices are costly to ecosystems and heavily impact soils, water and the atmosphere, as well as reducing biodiversity, as the world population reaches 7 billion, the burden of large scale agricultural production of meat and the energy consumption involved, will accelerate pressures on the Earth's resources and ecosystems exponentially, beyond the tipping point. Therefore, we must return to organic farming practices that take into account biodiversity conservation and minimal environmental impact. How organic agriculture contributes to global food production has been subject to intense debate over the past decade. [5]Recent pioneering research at Berkeley University, which showed that the previous theories of Organic food production are not as efficient in comparison to conventional large scale industrial farming, is being challenged.

"In terms of comparing productivity among the two techniques, this paper sets the record straight on the comparison between organic and conventional agriculture.

"With global food needs predicted to increase greatly in the next 50 years, it is critical to look more closely at organic farming, because aside from the environmental impacts of industrial agriculture, the ability of synthetic fertilisers to increase crop yields has been declining." - Claire Kremen is professor of environmental science, policy and management and co-director of the Berkeley Food Institute.

According to the study's lead author, Lauren Ponisio, *"This is especially true if we mimic nature by creating ecologically diverse farms that harness important ecological interactions like the nitrogen-fixing benefits of inter-cropping or cover-cropping with legumes.''*

Organic farming is not inefficient, it is our lack of understanding and knowledge of how to maximise yields that is inefficient. Through education and permaculture training, it is possible to change agricultural practices to be more environmentally friendly and see organic farming harvests as being just as satisfactory to the needs of local communities.

By comparison, over a decade of unbiased scientific data has shown that Genetically Modified Organisms (GMOs), and their accompanying pesticides and fertilisers are not only detrimental to local biodiversity, but also to human health causing cancer and severe organ damage and digestive problems in human health. In a famous comprehensive two year study published in [6]"Food and Chemical Toxicology" researchers led by Gilles-Eric Seralini from the independent French Research Group - CRIIGEN, found that rats fed on a diet containing NK603 Roundup tolerant GM maize or given water containing Roundup, at levels permitted in drinking water and GM crops in the US, developed cancers faster and died earlier than rats fed on a standard diet. They suffered breast cancer and severe liver and kidney damage. Within hours of the published papers findings, there was a rain of backfiring letters and complaints from pro GMO stakeholders and scientists. The UK's Science Media Centre, an organisation that defends and promotes GM technology has taken funding from GMO companies like Monsanto and Syngenta, led a vehement campaign to discredit one of the most detailed and thorough studies ever done on a GM food and its associated pesticide.

According to *GMO Myths and Truths*, a recently published 300 page report by Genetic Engineering scientist John Fagan, PhD *et al*, Séralini's critics soon turned their attention to putting pressure on to get the journal which had published the study to retract it. However, most of these unsubstantiated accusations were being made by people that had undisclosed conflicts of interest with the GM industry or industry-funded lobby groups or with organisations with vested interests in public acceptance of GM technology. The study was also dismissed by regulatory agencies, including the European

Food Safety Authority (EFSA); these were the same agencies which had previously approved GM foods as safe.

From an ecological perspective, genetically modified species are detrimental to biodiversity conservation as genetic material may affect other species negatively, and again, insufficient studies were carried out before GMOs have been released into the environment ignoring their environmental impact. We live with GM crops and GM material in food production and it will be a number of years before we see the full impact of these effects on the environment but we are already seeing the effects on human health of consuming foods with genetically modified materials in them.

To address alternatives to Roundup and other toxic pesticides, a new and wonderful organic alternative will be available in the future thanks to the pioneering work of [8]Paul Stamets who is a world leading expert on Mycology. He has found a way to use fungi to keep insects from destroying crops and this means he holds the patent to the first successful eco-friendly pesticide control. His product is called SMART pesticides. These pesticides provide safe and permanent solutions for controlling over 200,000 species of insects, a patent that could put a large financial dent in Monsanto and other pesticide chemical producing giants. This patent has potential to revolutionise the way in which humans grow crops, if his environmentally friendly product is made available to agriculture without any hindrance from conventional competition. The work of Stamets doesn't stop there. He has discovered countless other revolutionary uses of mushrooms that are possible solutions for the world's problems. Mushrooms can clean up oil spills, restore habitats, and treat against pox and flu viruses to producing a new form of ecological fuel from mycelium sugars, called 'Econol'.

We are leaving our children to inherit an environment that we have turned into an open air laboratory, with no regard to the negative environmental impacts of genetically modified organisms and geo-engineering, the full consequences and combination of these two on the environment are already of great concern to independent scientists and researchers and both could be the reason why we are seeing mass deaths of plants, insects, birds and animals.

After working as an ecologist for thirteen years, one thing I am certain of is that the environmental crisis is a crisis of human consciousness. Nothing I or my fellow environmental conservationists do externally can be sustained for the long-term future. The problem will continue because the root of what is unfolding before us is a reflection of the corruption within governance, corporations and economy and a denial of our ecological relationship with the Earth. The root cause therefore, must be addressed in order to see any external transformation.

Environmental exploitation, human exploitation or war and violence cannot be solved by anything we do externally; the results will not be sustained long-term unless we fully understand that these issues reflect our misunderstanding of the world and ourselves in relation to it. War is an internal process associated with fear in the ego-mind that fuels greed and power and exploitation is an internal process arisen from delusions of superiority, dissatisfaction, separation, humiliation, anger and pain. Our state of internal being is somewhat fragmented as a result of humanity believing that we are separate or superior to nature, this in itself is an idea that carries violence to ourselves, to the Earth and to our fellow species.

We are nature, our human bodies are comprised of communities of individual cells working in harmony to make possible our functioning organs and human body. We can only live if our individual cells work in harmony to function as a whole. That is why we are nature and in that respect, as [7]Cell Biologist, Bruce Lipton, always highlights in his work- we have a lot to learn from studying cells and how they function. When a single cell starts dysfunctional behaviour, it is usually when it operates only for the good of itself, rather than the good of the community of cells it is part of, this is when malfunctioning cells can become cancerous or create health problems. We as human beings have become a threat to ourselves, one another, fellow species and the Earth because many of us are operating on self-serving values rather than values for the good of our communities, our fellow species or for the good of the planet. We are wonderful when we can defend and nurture our individuality, though if we become selfish and greedy at the expense and suffering of other species, the environment, and other people, we can only do harm to ourselves and others. We are a part of the macro-ecology (natural ecosystems and the grander scale of nature), if we continue to be irresponsible, not re-prioritising our values and neglecting internal awareness, this undoubtedly reflects as a manifestation on our external environment.

We are unified with the ecology of nature, we are part of its ecology, and we are not separate from our external environment. We are deeply connected to the external world by our inner thought processes, perceptions and emotions and ultimately by our actions. Everything that goes on internally is manifested externally through our concept of ourselves in relation to our environment and others. This is what current research in quantum physics and new advanced fields in biology are discovering. When we have become more aligned with our hearts and souls internally and taken responsibility of all aspects of these internal processes, only then will we achieve outward peace and harmony for the Earth, environment and humanity.

"We cannot win this battle to save species and environments without forging an emotional bond between ourselves and nature as well - for we will not fight to save what we do not love" Stephen Jay Gould (1991).

A new sustainable Earth requires a reboot of human consciousness from a corrupt hierarchical pyramid structure driven by greed, to a multi-dimensional holographic transformation that embraces our union with all life on Earth and in the Cosmos. We cannot categorise the healing work that is required for either healing nature or healing the human, the two cannot be separated. We are one, therefore we need to treat ourselves as one, the outer world is only a reflection of inner consciousness, there is much we need to re-address of ourselves, and this is one aspect of the values in deep ecology.

Sustainability empowers the planet and people. That is the only way for humanity to have a chance of survival. This change can happen if communities take it into their own hands to build new sustainability blueprints. We cannot wait any longer to make the choice or wait for governments to choose for us. They will never serve for humankind's best interests. The clock has stopped ticking and we need to choose which direction in the forked road to take, only one decision is going to help us survive and a sustainable economy that takes into account the Earth's natural carrying capacity within the means of her natural resources is the only option from here on.

The Corporate take over of politics is driving global ecocide. The entire economy can be rebuilt on principles within the limits of the Earth's natural resources, with strict parameters being applied to energy giants and corporations, so that they cannot exploit our last great wildernesses for short-term gain. To do this, much re-arranging within governments would be required. Ideally, conservationists and ecological economists, sustainability experts and environmental law makers should be given political powers to become appropriate candidates to fill the seats in governments worldwide to replace the current oil barons, pharmaceutical and biotechnological stakeholders in governments that are destroying the environment and human health with their corporations, along with bankers and elite with their privileges above natural law. [9]The Rights of Nature should be one of the highest values that an evolved civilised society upholds, not the destruction of the environment for money and power; everything is currently upside down and inside out when it comes to values and morals in society. Let us envision how we would like to see the Earth and human society in 20 years' time. Now is a time where this hope relies on individuals who are willing to take responsibility to make changes in their own lives, to contribute to building bridges to a more sustainable future. We can each make daily commitments towards this vision, this is where we can shape opportunity out of crisis.

Einstein once remarked, "*We can't solve problems by using the same kind of thinking we used when we created them.*" The process of building a better world must begin with rethinking basic assumptions and exploring solutions for the root causes. Sustainability was born out of the ecology movement, in Ecology we have a term called '*Carrying Capacity*'. A population can live within the means of Earth's natural carrying capacity, but when a species goes beyond it, it usually results in extinction of the population or some sort of bottleneck which has a profound impact on the environment, species survival and its gene pool health and conservation. Sustainability for mankind is about living within the realistic means of the Earth's natural carrying capacity. Our oligarchic government and corporations do not wish to see the red margin lines, they act as if there are no limits by which we are constrained, because they are acting for a self-serving agenda, they continue to ignore all the warning signs.

To understand what the benefits of sustainability are, we need to take a look at the bigger picture in which Capitalism is the driving force for present day human society, economics and political decisions. It isn't all bad in that it encourages high standards in society through competition, culture, music, art, technology, production and economy, but we are failing by ignoring the building of high standards in environmental protection, ethics and management. Ironically, one reason is that pollution makes politicians money, and that is in addition to the millions which they already receive through lobbying agencies funded by oil companies in order to influence political decisions and policies which is a legalized form of bribery. There are many clues that point towards this; for example, it is well known to people who work in the oil industry operating in the Amazon, that when an oil spill occurs, the person who did the spilling gets an insurance pay off to clean up the mess, but the cleaning process is initially almost as toxic as the spill itself and many of these oil people 'accidentally' spill in order to receive the pay off. Corporations such as Oil and Biotechnological companies and politicians, all get similar insurance pay offs for environmental catastrophes, the environment however just gets destroyed.

It took me a decade of research to stumble upon some amazing solutions for sustainable and clean energy living, the big question for me as an environmental biologist was why were governments not implementing any of these strategies? Especially if they were aware of them, since so many patents to clean energy technologies have been documented.

The oligarchy only care about maintaining power, not maintaining a sustainable planet for mankind. Capitalism not only creates competition but it leans more towards corporate monopolisation and energy monopolisation which creates further corruption in governments because the corporations with extra money, contribute it to the politicians whom they want to influence to change (rewrite) environmental protection policies, and so to allow these energy giants to destroy natural wildernesses and people's health in the process. Governments can no longer continue to centralise control over the Earth's natural resources, water in India should be managed by Indians, water in Africa by Africans and so on, and not be under management by some distant French Water company that makes a fortune out of privatisation and thereby making life harder for the poor who live in developing countries. Human rights have been vastly exploited in the developing world due to lack of corporate social and ecological responsibilities. When the western world attempts to manage another country's resources it fragments communities and causes large scale ecocide in a detached way without seeing the consequences much like an air pilot releasing bombs over a foreign city to fly off without seeing the results or being aware of the civilian deaths. Local people have a right to manage local resources, it is a human right which has been taken away from local governments and the key to success of any conservation project is by allowing local people to manage their own resources, when to plant maize, when to harvest coffee, when to go fishing, after all, they are the ones that know their land better than some investment banker sipping coffee in his New York Penthouse.

When we start caring for one another and working for a sustainable environment, it binds and repairs communities. There is a lot of community spirit here in Ecuador; nothing promotes community spirit more than localised food production, as it relies on a strong community that cares about how its food is produced with maximum healthy productivity. Sustainability already exists here on many levels, as living off the land is natural to many Ecuadorians, the majority of the population are campesinos, farmers and indigenous people, who cultivate much of their food in a very sustainable way, producing an amazing variety of foods and alternative health products with rainforest herbal medicine which is also encouraged in Ecuador and which currently enjoys a degree of government protection.

ENDNOTES: Chapter 1.

1. The Science Journal, Planetary Boundaries: Guiding Human Development on a Changing Planet (Will Steffen, Katherine Richardson, Johan Rockström, Sarah E. Cornell, Ingo Fetzer, Elena M. Bennett, Reinette Biggs, Stephen R. Carpenter, Wim de Vries, Cynthia A. de Wit, Carl Folke, Dieter Gerten, Jens Heinke, Georgina M. Mace, Linn M. Persson, Veerabhadran Ramanathan, Belinda Reyers, Sverker Sörlin. 19 Feb. 2015).

2.Geo-engineering information-

a) Chad M Briggs, Ph.D. (24 Jan 2013) "*Is Geoengineering a National Security Risk?*" Global Interconnections LLC Global Int Working Paper #2.

b) Eli Kintisch."*DARPA to Explore Geoengineering*". Science Insider (14th March, 2009).

c) Alan Robock, Luke Oman, Georgiy L. Stenchikov (16th August, 2008) "*Regional climate responses to geoengineering with tropical and Arctic* SO_2 *injections*". Journal of Geophysical Research-Atmospheres. .

d) Bonnheim, Noah Byron (18th Oct. 2010) "*History of climate engineering.*" John Wiley.

e) Yusoff K, (2013) "The geoengine: geoengineering and the geopolitics of planetary modification" *Environment and Planning* **45** (12) 2799 – 2808

3. The IUCN Redlist is the most comprehensive list of the world's species that are endangered, it is a continual growing list of animal and plant species that scientists add to, from scientific studies conducted all over the world with data collected via biodiversity surveys. The IUCN can be visited here http://www.iucnredlist.org/photos/2014

4. Helena Norberg Hodge profile at the International Forum on Globalisation http://ifg.org/helena-norberg-hodge/

5. Berkeley University Studies on Organic Produce Yields vs Industrial Agricultural Yields, available online

6. GMO information-

a) Report available for free download by John Fagan, PhD; Michael Antoniou, PhD; Claire Robinson, MPhil (19th May 2014) "*GMO Myths and Truths*". Second edition, Published by Earth Opensource. http://earthopensource.org/gmomythsandtruths/

b) Gilles-Eric Séralinia, Emilie Claira, Robin Mesnagea, Steeve Gressa, Nicolas Defargea, Manuela Malatestab, Didier Hennequinc, Joël Spiroux de Vendômoisa (November, 2012) "*Long term toxicity of a Roundup herbicide and a Roundup-tolerant genetically modified maize.*" Food and Chemical Toxicology. Elsevier. Volume 50, Issue 11, Pages 4221–4231

c) Committee for Independent Research and Information on Genetic Engineering. www.criigen.org

7. Dr Bruce Lipton (2005) "*The Biology of Belief*" Hay House UK.

8. World leading Mycologist expert Paul Stamets has produced environmentally pesticides from fungi-website - http://www.fungi.com/about-paul-stamets.html

9. The Global Alliance for the Rights of Nature- http://therightsofnature.org

Chapter 2: Making Money out of Hot Air-Carbon Trading.

So you believe in Global Warming, (GW)? The media and governments have engineered a consensus that the Earth's rising temperatures are going to be the end of us all. Here is a bit of information that you might consider to understand the bigger picture, and why politicians call the rest of us GW scientific sceptics '*heretics*', '*deniers*' or '*conspiracy theorists*'. The GW debate is not just about governments using and manipulating scientific data to make trillions on trading carbon on the stock market, it is being used as a social engineering tactic to manipulate, divide, coerce and distract good people like environmental scientists, campaigners and non-governmental foundations and activists that could be putting their energy together to pressure governments to stop repressing Free Energy systems but good people are instead being directed into supporting much worse agendas which they themselves are unaware of -

a) For government financial gain through Carbon tax and Carbon trading,

b) For severe repressive sanctions that increase poverty and suffering of people in developing nations and that impede the development and growth of '*third*' world continents like Africa, Asia and India, (so that the '*first world*' nations can continue to control and plunder the natural resources and conflict minerals, (gold, diamonds and minerals) using slave labour in these countries, while the West continues to pollute the environment more than some of these countries do, yet they are the ones that have to comply to unrealistic sanctions).

c) For Geoengineering, an excuse to reign a global experiment of a previously untested toxic cocktail of chemicals and nano-particles on people and nature, in the name of '*cooling the planet*', which is polluting **soils** and **oceans** and contaminating natural **fresh water** sources, killing **trees** and **bees**.

d) To tighten control the world's water reserves and resources, to orchestrate a scarcity of water to increase prices of domestic water usage to make money and exploit people's need of a basic human right.

Real environmental scientists take into account unbiased scientific data from analysis of Sun spot activity, to air trapped in ice cores and weather balloons and from tree rings or geological records, all of which show the planet has been heating and cooling far longer than we have been able to measure life on Earth. Basically, the science on Global Warming is not settled, there are thousands of climate and environmental scientists who do not support the GW Alarmist theory, the scientific data that governments use is not scientific, it is manipulated and changed by governments before being presented to the public and the United Nations are involved in the agenda, they use erroneous climate models based on flawed assumptions instead of relying on empirical data. We do not accept that we are doomed to extinction because temperatures will soar to alarming rates based on erroneous climate models.

Despite this, environmental scientists know we are in a *desperate* environmental crisis **now.** We are living in an unfolding ecocide driven by government corruption and corporate greed and the destruction of the natural environment by powerful oil companies to drill for gas and oil. It is well known to climate and environmental scientists, that we have had temperatures rise far higher than they are today for over 15,000 years, even as far back as 450, 000 years, through wholly natural causes, as the following graph demonstrates.

This graph is based on the scientific method of measuring CO_2 in ice cores over the last ten thousand years. Ice cores are a great way to study climate as little air bubbles get trapped when the ice was formed, so the ice acts like virtual time capsule archives for global gasses and temperatures that date back over thousands of years.

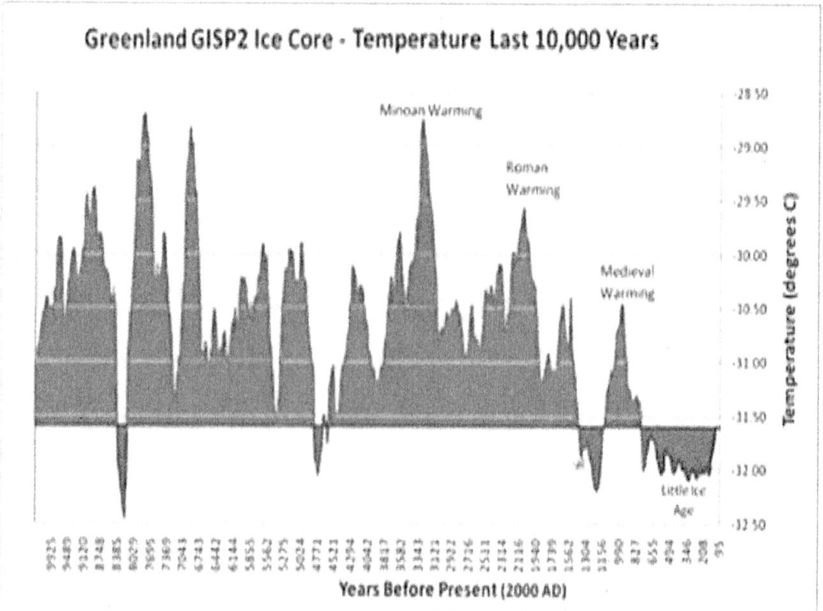

[1]Graph A. Shows Climate Change over the last 10,000 years to have reached higher and lower levels than today, data from the Vostock Ice cores.

Global Warming is not going to end life on Earth and it has only ever been a political and social engineering scam. The general public have been duped, and the only reason is so that politicians and banks can make money out of thin air and reign tight control on other developing countries. In fact, banks and politicians have been making trillions out of trading carbon credits since 2006, while pretending to care for the environment, yet they still get their big oil maintenance payoffs for rewriting environmental laws which allow the fossil fuel industry to continue to boom and the environment to continue to be destroyed, whilst actively repressing countless clean energy alternatives that are reliable and usable.

The unbiased scientific data in the graphs taken from the Vostock Ice cores shows cooling trends as well as warming trends throughout history before the industrial era and before humans were '*civilised*', if we can call ourselves that yet. One thing is certain, and that is that the climate is changing but as anyone who has studied environmental science will be aware, this is completely normal, though it may not be natural with the geoengineering and weather manipulation that is operating on a covert level.

Carbon dioxide is said to be a pollutant, the 'greenhouse gas' that politicians, the media and NGOs blame for global warming. It is a relatively minor greenhouse gas and is a product of natural ecology and life processes occurring on the planet, therefore it is not a pollutant (apart from the industrial emissions that humans contribute which again is minor in comparison to naturally produced CO2 which gets sequestered back into the soils, oceans, geology and ecosystems), and according to authentic non-biased climate data, there is no evidence of global temperatures being increased by an increase in carbon dioxide concentration. In the list of CO_2 sources and emissions on Earth, Volcanoes come first by a long way. Animals and insects come second, and industrial man follows as a very poor third contributor. CO_2 makes up only 0.036% of the atmosphere. A few years ago, an engineer friend of mine, calculated that all of the vehicles on all of the roads in all of the countries of the world produced about 1.7% of man's fairly limited contribution to man-made emissions.

Professor John Christy is a professor of atmospheric science at the University of Alabama in Huntsville. He was in fact, an editor and contributor to a section of the 2001 report of the United Nations Intergovernmental Panel on Climate Change. And yet, his paper was one of the 33 papers which were mostly ignored out of the 45 papers submitted by climate scientists. In 1991 he was awarded NASA's medal for scientific achievement, and in 1996, he received a special award from the American meteorological society for fundamentally advancing our ability to monitor climate. Although data observations show that ground temperatures have an increase, Dr Christy noted that the rise in temperature in the upper part of the atmosphere is not at all dramatic, and that does not match the results which climate models are producing at the moment, this is possibly due to the implication that the climate models are built on flawed assumptions such as carbon dioxide leading temperatures to rise, which is not actually true, the Ice core records show temperature rises *before* not after CO^2. Christy points out that the weather balloon data and satellite data both show that surface temperatures are rising slightly but the upper atmospheric air temperatures are not rising by any significant amount. This evidence shows that the hypothesis of man-made global warming is wrong. [2] Though Dr. Christy has been dismissed in environmental circles as a pawn of the fossil-fuel industry who distorts science to fit his own ideology, "*I don't take money from industries*," he said.

It is an oxymoron that the environmentalists do not realise that governments earn trillions from trading carbon credits at the same time as repressing diverse clean energy alternatives. Carbon trading has done nothing to reduce real carbon emissions or do the non-governmental organizations or environmental campaigners know that oil companies pay politician decision makers to bend the environmental policies and rules for fuel companies. Environmentalists are really working to keep the GW illusion for politicians and bankers to get rich. Yet politicians keep talking about what we need to do to prevent Global Warming. Environmental activists and non-governmental organizations need to focus on the more pressing issues such as the lack of legislation in international environmental law to implement strong boundaries of protection against super corporations exploiting the natural environment. Laws that are desperately needed to protect our last wild places and National Parks which are increasingly being invaded by mining and fossil fuel extraction companies, we need strong global environmental laws to protect biodiversity on earth and stop ecocide. We need laws to protect the availability of alternative clean energy inventions that are currently prevented from being on the available market simply because the oligarchy cannot make millions from them, yet these alternatives are the answer to the energy and environmental crisis problem. This is the crisis that is affecting international security of peace and future survival of mankind and of life this planet. This is what needs to be the crucial focus for activists and environmental campaigners, however instead people are wasting a lot of time and money funding the GW agenda.

[3] Professor Ian Clark, Department of Sciences, University of Ottawa is an arctic paleo-climatologist, he looked at carbon dioxide extracted from ice cores, isolated and analysed, showing decades to hundreds of years of carbon data readings. The results of his investigation show that the connection between temperature and carbon dioxide is, in fact, the opposite to what the governments and their message conveyors the media are saying, he is also saying that the current climate models used are mostly erroneous.

"If you haven't understood the climate system, if you haven't understood all the components -- the cosmic rays, the solar, the CO_2, the water vapour, the clouds, and put it all together -- if you haven't got all that, then your model isn't worth anything." As in most computer models, the adage of "junk in -- junk out" remains true for climate models''.—Professor Ian Clark.

Climate Modelling is not based on empirical scientific data collection, it is based on theoretical model projections, it is complicated and is usually based on short-term analysis to make long-term predictions, short-term analysis is generally unreliable and unable to produce meaningful long-term forecasts. This is disagreeable for pro Global Warming thinkers, because long-term modelling does not reflect Global Warming. In addition to models not taking into account cosmic rays, the sun's activity, cloud cover and the water vapour, the biased towards Anthropogenic Global Warming, (AGW), has set back any unbiased developments of climate modelling by decades. A report published in 2009 on current Climate Models states-

[4]*'Previously known and accepted climate components have been summarily stripped from the equation such as the dominant factors involving the Sun and the importance of water vapour in the atmosphere as the dominant greenhouse gas. This is because in the cause to acquire lucrative AGW-biased government grants, many scientists have opted to skew their climate models blatantly to amplify AGW - favouring evidence and amplifying anthropogenic*

CO_2 importance. In this manner, they then qualify to receive funding and ensure publication.

'Describing the compounded inaccuracies of these Johnny-come-lately modellers who would rather be funded than be scientifically accurate, Dr. Tim Ball, a former climate scientist at the University of Winnipeg sardonically clarifies: "The analogy that I use is that my car is not running that well, so I'm going to ignore the engine (which is the sun) and I'm going to ignore the transmission (which is the water vapour) and I'm going to look at one nut on the right rear wheel (which is the Human produced CO2) ... the science is that bad!"- Gregory Young.

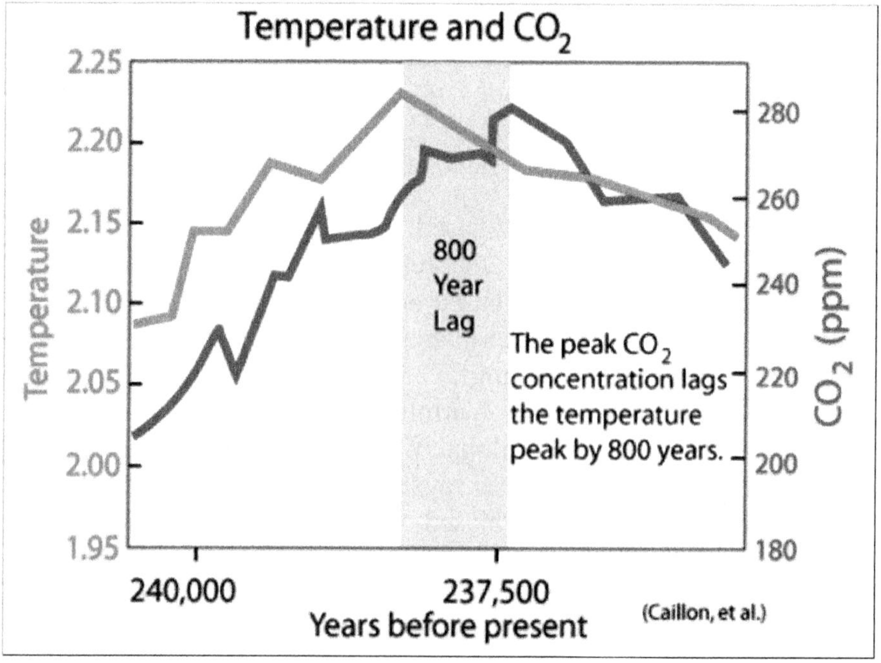

[1]Graph B) Shows the 800 year lag of CO_2 behind temperature rises **based on** .Vostock ice core data.

[1]The Carbon Dioxide Information Analysis Centre (CDIAC) states that according to Barnola et al. (1991) and Petit et al. (1999) the CO_2 measurements taken from the deepest Ice Core samples indicate that, at the beginning of the de-glaciations, increase either was in phase or lagged by less than ~1000 years with respect to the Antarctic

temperature, whereas it clearly lagged behind the temperature at the onset of the glaciations. What this means is global temperatures increased **before** the level of Carbon dioxide rose. There is an actual **eight hundred year lag** between global temperature rising or falling before the concentration of Carbon dioxide follows it. This shows that temperature rise leads Carbon dioxide concentration by eight hundred years. Please understand clearly that Carbon dioxide concentration is **caused by** global temperature, it does not **cause** a rise in global temperature. These results show up time and again over different unrelated ice core surveys. Unfortunately, most climate change computer models are wrong because they are based on the mistaken belief that Carbon dioxide causes global temperatures to rise which is wholly incorrect. This raises the question; are the climate modellers *paid* to come up with such ridiculous results or are they really that stupid?

One of the key ecosystems in global climate is the ocean. Its micro-organisms generate 80 percent of the world's oxygen gas. The oceans also soak up Carbon dioxide when temperatures drop and release that Carbon dioxide again when temperatures rise once more. Solar activity has more to do with influencing temperature rises than anything we are doing. According to astrophysicists, variations in Sun spot activity correlates and synchronises with Earth's temperature fluctuations.

The fundamental assumption that Carbon dioxide causes a rise in temperature is **wrong**. Yet why has such data been manipulated and publicised? The political and financial world make about several trillion dollars per year from carbon 'trading'. The funding for climate science into global warming is around 170 million dollars a year, the fundamental lie has generated income for global warming campaigns and non-profit organisations and hundreds of jobs have been created out of this fake assumption which ignores the real scientific data.

Science was never meant to be corrupted or manipulated by politicians and governments, it was meant to provide objective unbiased and honest data, but yet again, human nature has taken it upon itself to manipulate science for the personal gain of those whom have the means and power to become richer than they already are. Politics and policy makers have no right to mess with science in order to make money.

Global temperatures are not rising exponentially, ground level temperatures may show some changes and rising. Temperatures in some countries have risen at ground level but not at upper atmospheric levels, upper atmospheric temperatures is where real climate scientists get their empirical data from and this is what 33 scientists have shown in data ignored by the IPCC report which has been the basis for every final government endorsed conclusion. This media-endorsed political hype using falsified science is continually used in published stories on soaring temperatures of land and oceans, but the journalists producing these stories have not based their claims on any genuine scientific data.

Changes in sea level caused by movements in the Earth's crust or from melting of glaciers take more than a human lifetime of data to be detected in measurements of temperature changes, and though the newspapers claim otherwise, sea temperatures in only a few parts of world have risen with surface temperature. No real data shows a correlation between sea level temperatures worldwide and those areas that show ocean rises, such as off the Californian coast needs to be investigated to show that there is no connection to the Fukushima nuclear radiation affecting the temperature of the Pacific Ocean. Oceans naturally absorb CO_2 as well as releasing it. That is a natural cycle which has been going on since life on Earth began.

There is no correlation between ground temperatures and upper Earth atmosphere temperatures. The ground temperature readings show a rise in temperature in some geographical areas but the upper atmosphere temperature are not rising significantly. Understanding that this is where global warming caused by greenhouse gasses is supposed to take place, it is odd that this data is completely ignored by governments.

I encourage the reader, to do further research and make up your own mind, my concern is that the public is being duped yet again by governments and banking firms such as Goldman Sachs which has made trillions from carbon trading. [3]The first Carbon Credit trading system started in Europe in 2005. It wasn't until 2008 that the US realised what a great monopoly it was, Goldman Sachs paid $3.5 million to lobby (legally bribe) politicians to push for global warming issues. The US Democratic Party received $4,452,585 from Goldman Sachs to push into "environmental plans", called 'cap-and-trade'. The carbon-credit market was born thereafter and is a virtual repeat of the commodities-market casino that's been lucrative to bankers and politicians. Cap-and-trade, as envisioned by Goldman Sachs, is really just a carbon-tax structured so that private interests collect the revenues. Instead of simply imposing a fixed government levy on pollution emissions and forcing polluting energy producers to pay for the mess which they make; cap-and-trade allows a small group of Wall Street elite to exploit allegedly environmentally friendly disguised tax into a private tax-collection scheme. It allows the banks and political stakeholders to seize taxpayer money before it's even collected. So while governments pretend to care about environmental problems, make sure you follow the money and do the research before every environmental policy is set forth, always ask the question, - is this really for the benefit of the environment or is it for those in positions of power to make big money?

''Unlike traditional commodities, which at some time during the course of their market exchange must be physically delivered to someone, carbon credits do not represent a physical commodity but instead have been described as 'a legal fiction that is poorly understood by many sellers, buyers and traders'. This lack of understanding makes carbon trading particularly vulnerable to fraud and other illegal activity. Carbon markets, like other financial markets, are also at risk of exploitation by criminals due to the large amount of money invested, the immaturity of the regulations and lack of oversight and transparency'' - [4]Interpol

The general public needs to be aware of, or at least attempt to investigate for themselves the reasons why politicians and the elite benefit from making people *believe* in Global Warming. One other benefit to the oligarchy is controlling water as a monopoly and the Bush family bought all of Paraguay's fresh largest body of aquifer water earlier this decade.

Despite my presenting an argument against the Global Warming hype, one of the potent messages of this book is to show the reader that if we continue using fossil fuels as we are doing at present, we can only bring doom and destruction on ourselves and the future of the planet. Drilling, fracking and mining are largely responsible for ecocide. Politics have been taken over by big oil, not just in the USA, but also in Europe and the UK. I stumbled upon a revealing report by the [5]Sierra Club, whilst I was trying to figure out what is happening in politics for the environmental agreements and policies to be getting worse rather than better. This report illustrates an uncomfortable reality for Americans that care about protecting the health of the environment and communities by showing that the nation's biggest polluters are increasing their political spending and seeing even better returns on their investment than ever before. The report shows that the payoff for big polluters is very real, and is in the form of billions in tax subsidies, anti-regulatory policies, and distorted priorities that give the wealthiest corporations in the nation a way to drown out the concerned voices of everyone else who does care about the environment. This was the answer I was looking for to the reason why environmental laws in the USA and the UK are being eroded rather than reinforced therefore making the crisis far worse, allowing fracking and drilling to take place in previously protected conservation areas. These energy companies are so powerful that they can now use lobbying methods of legal bribes to pay off politicians and law makers to rewrite environmental policies to suit their needs. If this is not the only proof we need to scrap these undemocratic legal lobbying scams, is it not also evident that we are heading for environmental catastrophe, because the caring human has become extinct in a world of political bribery.

The other aspect of these political lies means that the elite can continue to repress third world countries and get 350 non-profit organizations, (NGOs) in on these repressive sanctions too. Despite the problems with unsettled science and errors in global climate models, the worst aspect of the so called Global Warming movement is that 350 NGOs are supporting Rockefeller led suppression and complete control of Africa and other third-world countries with signing up to ''emission cuts'', third world countries are affected by land grabs and sanctions that will put people into further deeper poverty, starvation and suffering for the next 50 years. One example is of a foundation serving as a front group for US industrialists; the CEO of Climate Works is [6]William K. Reilly. Prior to his position with Climate Works, Reilly served as the administrator of the U.S. Environmental Protection Agency, president of the World Wildlife Fund, president of The Conservation Foundation, and director of the Rockefeller Task Force on Land Use and Urban Growth, he has also headed the U.S. Delegation to the U.N. Conference on Environment and Development in Rio in 1992.

At the historic press conference which took place on November 11, 2009 in Copenhagen, Lumuma Di-Aping, the Sudanese diplomat whom was the chief negotiator for the G77 at that time, Di-Aping addressed the international NGO community. The conference room was brimming with representatives of the non-profit industrial sector and corporate media. In a most direct approach, Di-Aping asked non-government organizations to support the demand that developed countries cut emissions 52% by 2017; 65% by 2020; and 80% by 2030 (based on a 1990 baseline).

"The second issue is the issue of reductions of emissions. There must be radical reductions of emissions starting from now. In our view, by 2017 we should cut; developed countries must cut by 52%, 65% by 2020, 80% by 2030, well above 100 percent by 2050. And this is very important because the more you defer action the more you condemn millions of people to immeasurable suffering. So the idea that you start from 4% today and you achieve 80 or 50 in 2050 simply means that you do not care about the lives of those who will be devastated in this period, until you pick up the pace."

"... and I will say this to our colleagues from Western civil society (environmental campaigners and activists) — *you have definitely sided with a small group of industrialists and their representatives and your representative branches. Nothing more than that. You have become an instrument of your governments. Whatever you say, whether you think it's because it's tactically shrewd or not, it's an error that you should not continue to make.*"- [7]Di-Aping.

Instead of using coal, oil and fossil fuels which are posing serious problems for large scale ecocide just through their extraction and on people's health through their emissions, we must replace those fossil fuels with sustainable, alternative energy. The main reason why the Amazon Rainforest is so critically in danger of disappearing over the next few decades is because of oil drilling and mining. Species of animals and plants worldwide are disappearing at a rate of up to150 species per day. However, all ecosystems are critically in danger and environmental campaigners are worrying about fictitious temperature rises. I part with this information because I am dedicated to truth, so many good environmental campaigners have put a lot of their free time and energy into helping politicians get richer out of the Global Warming hype and support them in pushing sanctions to make poor countries suffer more, instead of the West cutting their own emissions. What justice is this and where are the real solutions? Instead, we can put our concerns and greatly needed actions to these other much graver environmental issues, campaigning to stop using oil, gas and nuclear power, let us remove the cause of pollutants altogether and work towards introducing alternative clean energy, let us invest our time and energy into ceasing the repression of this cause rather than arguing over whether temperatures are rising or falling.

ENDNOTES: Chapter 2.

1. a) The ice cores are unique with their entrapped gas and air inclusions enabling direct records of past changes in atmospheric trace-gas composition. Graph A and B shows Authentic data origin from the Vostock Ice Cores

Graph data from the Vostock Ice Core data here- http://cdiac.ornl.gov/ftp/trends/co2/vostok.icecore.co2

And http://cdiac.ornl.gov/ftp/trends/temp/vostok/vostok.1999.temp.dat

(From http://cdiac.ornl.gov/trends/co2/vostok.html)

b) Barnola, J.-M., P. Pimienta, D. Raynaud, and Y.S. Korotkevich (1991) *CO2-climate relationship as deduced from the Vostok ice core: A re-examination based on new measurements and on a re-evaluation of the air dating*. Tellus 43(B):83- 90.

c) Petit, J.R., Jouzel, J., Raynaud, D., Barkov, N.I., Barnola, J.-M., Basile, I., Bender, M., Chappellaz, J., Davis, M., Delaygue, G., Delmotte, M., Kotlyakov, V.M., Legrand, M., Lipenkov, V.Y., Lorius, C., Pepin, L., Ritz, C., Saltzman, E., and Stievenard, M. (1999). Climate *and atmospheric history of the past 420,000 years from the Vostock ice core*, Antarctica. Nature 399: 429-436.

d) Caillon, N., Severinghaus, J.P., Jouzel, J., Barnola, J.-M., Kang, J. and Lipenkov, V.Y (2003) Timing of atmospheric CO_2 and Antarctic temperature changes across Termination III. *Science* **299**: 1728-1731.

e) Mudelsee, M. 2001. The phase relations among atmospheric CO2 content, temperature and global ice volume over the past 420 ka. Quaternary Science Reviews 20: 583-589.

2 . Professor John Christy-

a) David H. Douglass, John R. Christy, Benjamin D. Pearson, S. Fred Singer, A (December, 2007) *Comparison of Tropical Temperature Trends with Model Predictions.* International Journal of Climatology, Volume 28, Issue 13, pp. 1693-1701.

b) Philip J. Klotzbach, Roger A. Pielke Sr., Roger A. Pielke Jr., John R. Christy, Richard T. McNider, (February 2009) *An Alternative Explanation for Differential Temperature Trends at the Surface and in the Lower Troposphere.* (Submitted to the Journal of Geophysical Research,

c) Michael Wines. (July 15th 2014) *Though Scorned by Colleagues, a Climate-Change Sceptic Is Unbowed.* New York Times,

d) John R. Christy, William B. Norris, Kelly Redmond, and Kevin P. Gallo, (2006) *Methodology and Results of Calculating Central California Surface Temperature Trends: Evidence of Human-Induced Climate Change? J. Climate*, **19**, 548–563. Doi. Volume 19, Issue 4

3.

a) Ian D. Clark, Jean-Charles Fontes. (May 1990), *Paleoclimatic reconstruction in northern Oman based on*

carbonates from hyper-alkaline ground waters. Quaternary Research
Volume 33, Issue 3, Pages 320–336

b) Tom Heinemann produced an excellent documentary called Carbon Crooks on the hidden corruption of Carbon trading in Denmark and internationally, you can find his documentary DVD for sale online.

4. Gregory Young. (March 31, 2009) *It's the Climate Warming Models, Stupid.* American Thinker.

5. Siera Club (March 10, 2014) *Polluting our Democracy and Our Environment.* Report Available online for free download.

6. a) Interpol International Police Investigation report (2012) "*Guide to Environmental Carbon Trading Crime*". Interpol. Available online for free download.

b) Information on the corruption behind 350 NGOs and the Rockafellas available at the website The Wrong Kind of Green.org

7. a) Lumumba Di-Aping of the G77. Minutes of meeting available on the website The Wrong Kind of Green. org

b) Lumumba's speech recorded under the title- *The Most Important COP Briefing the World Never Heard* Speech available online at YouTube

Chapter 3: Oil, Politics and the Amazon Rainforest

Firstly, in terms of conservation and ecology, the Amazon Rainforest produces around 20 percent of the world's oxygen and has a key role ecologically which should be in everyone's interest globally as insurance against climate instability. While we are on the subject of key ecosystems that contribute to oxygen production, although the Amazon rainforest is often referred to as 'the lungs of the Earth', it is the ocean's algae that produce 80 percent of the world's oxygen through photosynthesis, how is this possible? The oceans cover over 71 percent of the Earth's surface and the land consists of 29 percent. There are more than 7,000 different species of algae. Most live in the oceans, some occupy fresh water environments and others even live on land. Algae produce about 330 billion tons of oxygen each year. Therefore, it is the oceans that are the lungs of the Earth. Both of these key ecosystems are at tipping point and are currently threatened by Ecocide.

The Amazon is also precious in terms of water storage and run off, the Amazon River is over four thousand miles long and sixteen percent of the world's water runs through the Amazon, discharging into the Atlantic Ocean at Belém, Brazil, after emerging from the Peruvian Andes. The Amazon rainforest also releases around 8 trillion tons of water vapour to the atmosphere each year.

Secondly, the global reliance on oil makes all of us responsible for doing something to protect the Amazon, since the world's dependence on petroleum is one of the major causes of its rapid destruction, which again means the decisions for its conservation measures lay with the international community, not just with the Ecuadorian government or with the other countries that the Amazon occupies. Rainforests are the basis for more than 5,000 internationally consumed products from herbal medicines to food, furniture and clothing.

Thirdly, the Amazon is the largest rainforest in the world consisting of over 8 million square kilometres throughout nine countries. In the last ten years about 400,000 square kilometres of primary rainforest have been destroyed due to mineral and oil extraction and agricultural land use, such as cattle ranching, palm plantations and soy plantations.

In terms of time, it took 3,500 million years for the Amazon rainforest to evolve and grow into the species-rich biodiversity hotspot wonder of the world. If it is destroyed, then it is gone forever, nothing can replicate or replace that, short of another 3,500 million human-free years. The western part of the Amazon Basin is one of the richest biodiversity hotspots in the world; the level of biodiversity in the Ecuadorian Amazon is especially astounding. Just to put it into perspective, Yasuni national park contains around 600 species of birds and 170 species of mammals, 1,100 species of trees all in one quarter square kilometre area, and that is more species than in all of the U.S. and Canada, combined. Most people do not realise that much of the carbon released when a rainforest is destroyed is in the peat soil below the trees, it is not just in the trees but most of it is in the peat soils below which store thousands of tons of carbon, so they are invaluable carbon sinks, below the trees and this is key to help to regulating the climate. This means when deforestation occurs, all the carbon that was previously locked up in the peat soil below the rainforest is released into the atmosphere.

The *Convention on Biological Diversity* states that the Amazon contains more than 50 percent of the world's plant and animal species. We must not discount the value of its undiscovered secrets for medical science and for humankind, as already, people are discovering plant-based cures for cancer that come from rainforest plants, there are over 60,000 plant species in the Amazon and only 3 percent have been studied for medicinal properties. Many of our foods come from the rainforest along with other important materials. There are thousands of undiscovered species of plants and animals still in existence, but we are destroying them at a pace which is faster than we are discovering them. Therefore, everyone's opinion and actions are relevant and play on important role in defending this key ecosystem, as its devastation will be the devastation of all of us if we do not step in to defend what remains of the Amazon Rainforest.

Most people do not even think of where the oil they use in their cars come from, many think most oil wells are laid in some obscure desert on the ocean but much of the world's oil comes from the South American rainforest which not only is rich in oil but also in minerals, coal and gas. Due to the processes of the rainforest ecosystem there are huge oil reserves under the Amazon rainforest basin, which unfortunately only means one thing for the Amazon, ecosystem destruction. The Amazon rainforest is a major contributing ecosystem, yet there may be no Amazon forest left in twenty years if it continues to be destroyed due to the world's dependence on petroleum as one of the major causes of its rapid destruction. Much of the world's petroleum can be found underneath the rich peat soils built up from millions of years of compressed dead and organic plant and animal matter of tropical rainforests. Petroleum drilling and mineral extraction are the biggest environmental impact on rainforest conservation, oil drilling, which means thousands of kilometres of roads and pipelines have been built and inevitably oil spilled. Yet people do not think of rainforests when buying petrol for their cars and people have become desensitised to hearing the words "Save the Rainforest".

Before European settlers arrived in the Brazilian Amazon, the indigenous people numbered of more than 10 million across the Amazon Basin. The populations have since declined to less than 3 million, composed of four hundred different indigenous groups, half of which remain in Brazil.

[2]With every indigenous group that is decimated and every individual in a tribe, with every medicine man or woman that dies, a great wealth of knowledge of medicinal plants disappears with them. Each plant is a book of knowledge in terms of its biochemistry and medicinal properties.

When men destroy the Jungle, they've burned down a library of books without even having been able to read them" -Pablo Amaringo.

"Every time a Shaman dies, it is as if a library burned down" -Mark Plotkin.

Exploitation of Ecuador's Rainforest has been going on since the 1940s when previously uncontacted Waoarani territory was invaded, and now, oil production accounts for over 70 percent of Ecuador's exports, China being one of the biggest purchasers. [3]In 1967, The New York Times announced that a military style helicopter invasion by the Texaco-Gulf consortium similar to that deployed in Vietnam was used to invade territories to implement drilling rigs without the consent of the people at Lago Agrio, violating land titles and indigenous territory. [4]By the early 1970s, the largest oil pipeline of over 300 miles was laid. It went from the Amazon to the Andes and Esmeraldas, known as the Trans Ecuador pipeline, ten oil companies invaded and destroyed the Huoarani territories. Later in 1977, the Tihueno territory was invaded by an oil company but was met with fierce resistance, so the government sent in the military to kill the indigenous people, in most of these cases the indigenous people did not have much previous contact with the outside world. In 1979, Ecuador created Yasuni National Park and in 1989 it was declared a Bio reserve by UNESCO under the Man and Bio reserve programme, though this has done little to affect any strong conservation measures.

Texaco-Chevron had been drilling since 1963. Chevron saved money by intentionally by-passing environmental risk protocols which would have been normal legal procedure in the USA. In the process they destroyed the area of the Ecuadorian rainforest affecting five indigenous tribes and polluting their ancestral land and rivers with billions of gallons of oil and waste water over a number of years, waste that went into the Amazon Rivers and land surface, instead of pumping it back underground. These methods are deemed sub-standard and toxic to human and environmental health around the world. As a result during 1993, indigenous Ecuadorians took Texaco-Chevron to court over environmental and health damages after they had become victims of an on-going long-endured oil disaster, the likes of which had never been seen before: Compensation and environmental restoration still has not been received despite 18 years of legal battles with the people of Ecuador - some 30,000 indigenous people and mestizo (mixed ancestry) settlers. The Ecuadorian plaintiffs accused Texaco-Chevron, of dumping 18 billion gallons of toxic waste water and spilling about 17 million gallons of crude oil into the rainforest during its operations in Ecuador from 1964 to 1990. These illegal actions contaminated the soil, groundwater, rivers and streams in the area and this is still causing cancer, horrible congenital defects and abortions among the indigenous population. Another reason why oil spills are so commonplace in Ecuador is that they are carried out on purpose because there are insurance claims available and money for "cleaning up the spill".

[5]Dr Brian O'Leary was another expatriate very concerned about Ecuador's dependency on oil and lack of openness to embrace other cleaner energy initiatives. Before he died in 2011, I had some personal communication with Dr O'Leary on his vision for the Ecuadorian Initiative. He sent me this Initiative which was his vision, I want to share what he wrote, this is what he said:

"*Recently over 100 indigenous people occupying a bridge blocking the flow of oil company traffic deep in the Peruvian Amazon were slaughtered by helicopter gunships sent out by the president of Peru. The indigenous people of northern Amazonian Ecuador and Peru have suffered immeasurable environmental and health catastrophes at the hands of Chevron-Texaco and are pressing a multi-billion dollar lawsuit against the company for the utter devastation left behind in the rainforest. The native peoples of Peru, Ecuador and Bolivia are up in arms, determined not to allow these attacks on their homeland, and willing to fight to the death. The situation is reminiscent of nineteenth century U.S. seizures of Indian lands, followed by the utter destruction of their cultures. Meanwhile, the*

Ecuadorian government's ambiguous stance toward oil extraction, and the passing of draconian mining and water laws that allow multinational companies to come in and extract these non-renewable resources, have created a strong resistance from indigenous and poor people who are blocking roads and actually declaring war on the government in some quarters. Clearly, short of the total slaughter of the indigenous people, something on the government side has to give.

The moral imperative is clear: the temporary gain coming from a decade or two of extraction cannot possibly justify the destruction of an entire people and of a habitat considered to be irreplaceable. This kind of aggressive extraction is something that many corporate and governmental interests advocate, because their exclusive focus on short-term goals far outweighs their occasional thoughts about long-term sustainability.

"The dilemma here is that fast money can be made from drilling for oil, which is now the number-one export commodity of Ecuador. As the value of gold and other metals goes up, mining interests are increasing as well. The privatisation of water and its growing scarcity and impurity are also ominous trends. A moratorium on all these activities is the only way to achieve any kind of parity, consistent with the recent and globally unprecedented parts of the new Ecuadorian constitution providing for the rights of nature and the equality of indigenous nations." – Dr Brian O' Leary on the Ecuadorian Initiative

I was hoping to get the chance to work with O'Leary on developing a sustainability initiative but he died the very month that I arrived in Ecuador in 2011. He was one of the few scientists who also understood that alternative energy could be a key factor in helping stop rainforest destruction.

As life unfolds some of us may be fortunate to realise our childhood dreams, it can become a pivotal point in our lives, a significant event that leads to something more important. I have always been intrigued with the Amazon Rainforest ever since I was a young child. What made Ecuador appealing to me is the rainforest, living and working in the rainforest has been a dream of mine since I was a child, at the age of twelve years old, my bedroom was full of pictures of colourful rainforest animals and its people. I was constantly signing petitions or raising money for rainforest conservation or writing letters to famous naturalists like David Attenborough offering my humble services, if it was at all possible to become an apprentice or assistant. I wrote to countless organisations before I was even sixteen years old, asking to volunteer. I had a passion for animals and conservation; it really was a burning desire. During the month of August 2012, I had the privilege of venturing into the most remote area of the Ecuadorian Amazon to spend several weeks with the Shiwiar tribe, one of the rarer tribes in Ecuador. The territory is in Juintsa, about 7 hours in a canoe ride down the Amazon River to the Peruvian border. The Shiwiar people were extremely welcoming and some of the most hospitable indigenous people I have ever met in Ecuador.

Prior to this, I had been to work in other areas of the Ecuadorian Rainforest before but none as remote or unique as this. Everywhere you would see something surprising, groups of Red, Blue or Yellow Macaws flying in the tree canopies, monkeys playing in the branches, giant ants busily building their spectacular societies and at night you are treated to the most stunning display of stars accompanied by a chorus of singing frogs. All while biting insects are feasting on your arms and legs throughout the days and nights. I joked with my French biologist companions, that a biologist could measure the biodiversity of the rainforest by the variety of bites on one's body. The majesty and beauty of the Rainforest was worth every bit of the experience of living rough.

[6]On the fourth day of our visit, the tranquillity of the forest was interrupted by an uninvited military helicopter that landed in Juintsa

around the 21st of August. My heart began racing as we walked towards these intruders, there was only one thing I could think of why they were intruding upon the Shiwiar territory unannounced, 'Petroleum'. I warned the community, we went to talk to the officers whom claimed they were simply mapping the area as it had never officially been mapped before. I asked them if it was for oil, they denied it was. Little did I know that I was witness to the beginning of what could be the end of the Ecuadorian Amazon.

Military mapping Shiwiar territory, Juintsa.August.2012.Photo credit Carlita Shaw

After I recovered from Malaria and my Ecuadorian visa ran out, I returned to England in October 2012 and received some breaking news from one of my Shiwiar friends in Ecuador. Veronica Shiran, managed the Shiwiar radio station for the whole of northern Ecuador in the Pastaza region, she relayed to me, what was just announced to her community a few weeks ago, she said, "*what this means for the Shiwiar and for the other indigenous communities of the Amazon is beyond their worst nightmares*". On the 8th of August 2012,

President Rafael Correa entered into an agreement with The Ministry of Hydrocarbons and PetroPeru, to sell 15 Oil Block Reserves under over seventy-five thousand square kilometres of Primary Amazon Rainforest. This was only a portion of what later unfolded to be much larger sections of blocks being opened up for auction.

The Amazon is one of the most valuable biodiversity hotspots in the world, containing 50 percent of all life forms on this planet. Selling the last of the Ecuadorian Amazon to oil companies could transform Ecuador's rainforest into the largest operating oil field in the whole of the Amazon Basin, decimating biodiversity that has taken over 50 million years to evolve. The Amazon Rainforest is home to tens of thousands of plants, 2.5 million insect species, and some 2,000 birds and mammals. To date, at least 40,000 plant species, 2,200 fishes, 1,294 birds, 427 mammals, 428 amphibians, and 378 reptiles have been scientifically classified in the region and hundreds of thousands more are waiting to be discovered.

DECIMO PRIMERA RONDA PETROLERA Y TERRITORIOS INDÍGENAS

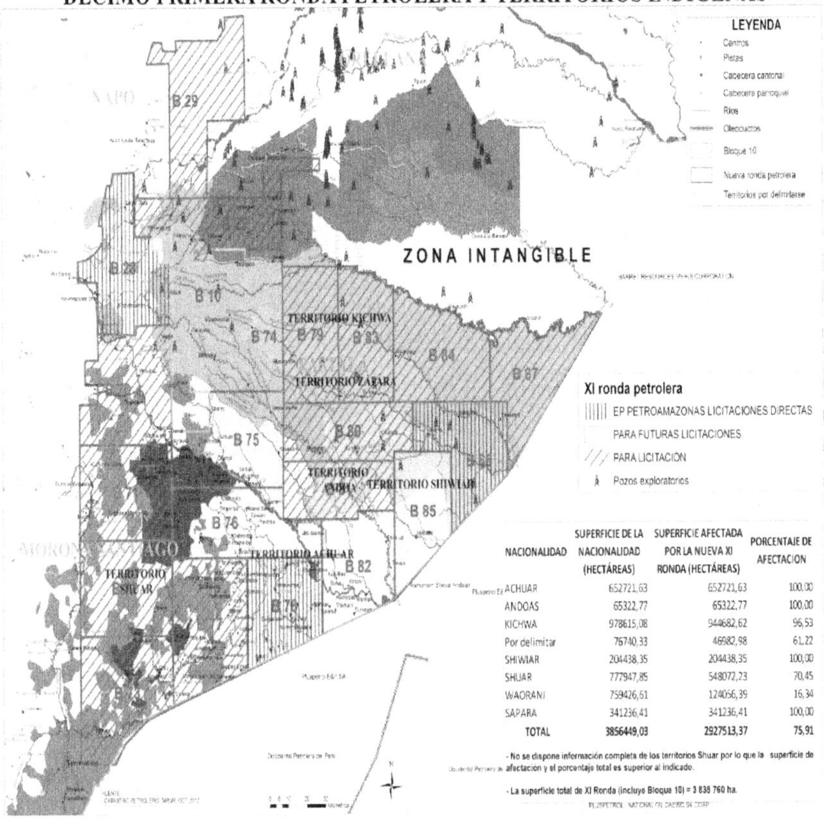

NACIONALIDAD	SUPERFICIE DE LA NACIONALIDAD (HECTÁREAS)	SUPERFICIE AFECTADA POR LA NUEVA XI RONDA (HECTÁREAS)	PORCENTAJE DE AFECTACION
ACHUAR	652721,63	652721,63	100,00
ANDOAS	65322,77	65322,77	100,00
KICHWA	978615,08	944682,62	96,53
Por delimitar	76740,33	46982,98	61,22
SHIWIAR	204438,35	204438,35	100,00
SHUAR	777947,85	548072,23	70,45
WAORANI	759426,61	124056,39	16,34
SAPARA	341236,41	341236,41	100,00
TOTAL	3856449,03	2927513,37	75,91

The above map lists all the different indigenous tribes of the Ecuadorian rainforest in the right hand box. The red squares are the oil blocks, Yasuni ITT is the area that is white and referred to as "Zona intangible", it is now also covered by oil blocks and oil drilling is taking place in Yasuni now, despite the efforts of ecologists and conservationists to protect Yasuni ITT.

Now the prospective areas of drilling stretches out to over eight hundred thousand square kilometres of primary tropical rainforest could be destroyed in the next few years by Oil Companies. President Correa forgot his responsibility to protect and care for the Amazon, to keep the oil reserves in the ground under the rainforest. Five years ago he made this promise to the world, to keep the Ecuadorian Amazon rainforest untouched, this not only applies to Yasuni National Park but to Pastaza and the rest of the Ecuadorian

Amazon. Correa's decision to sell the Amazon Rainforest to international Oil Companies shocked the world and will bring the end of the Ecuadorian Amazon and its indigenous people. For short-term economic gain, the environmental and humanitarian sacrifice is a heavy one to pay. The Ecuadorian Amazon is far more valuable environmental resource to its government and the rest of the world if kept preserved and untouched, sustainably and properly protected.

What will this mean to the Ecuadorian people, the end of forty years of peace perhaps? The environmental impact continues to be devastating, destroying the livelihoods and ancestral territories of hundreds of thousands of indigenous tribes. Seven indigenous tribes are being affected, the Kichwa, Sapara, Sarayaku, Shuar, Waorani, Shiwiar Andoas and Achuar. More indigenous villages will be displaced to make way for drilling, as they have done in other territories before such as at "Savaykwa" Kichwa territory, without permission, soldiers entered and started clearing people from their own land. This is a gross infringement of human rights, bringing the largest threat of indigenous population displacement and decimation since the country was invaded by Peru forty years ago.

Flying over the Ecuadorian Amazon, passing isolated tribes. August 2012. Photo credit Samual Remerand, friend and colleague.

Other repercussions may be disease and illness outbreaks amongst the indigenous such as cancer and cholera linked to irreversible environmental pollution as a result of further oil spills and considering the several uncontacted tribes, intrusion of their territories could be complete decimation for them. Respect to the Bolivian indigenous leader, President Evo Morales, he is an example to be followed by other world leaders, in 2012 he made a ban on genetically modified crops entering Bolivia and gave Planet Earth the same rights as a human being. After all, it makes sense when Earth provides us with everything we need to live.

Fifty million indigenous people live in the world's remaining forests and 370 million Indigenous people live in various different threatened wildernesses and ecological biomes across the world. We need to take into consideration, their defense treaties for the last natural wildernesses that they occupy on the Earth. I have found that working with indigenous people involves dealing with many of the front line issues that the larger established charities, governments and academic institutes have forgotten or know little about. The other great factor is that because many indigenous communities live solely off of the land, they are not motivated by money, many live in isolated regions that are difficult to access therefore they are not money motivated in the way Westerners are and this also goes in their favor to be the world's best and most trusted conservationists, their lives depend on the preservation and conservation of their ancestral land, not on money. Their connection with their environment is not just dependent on daily living; it is part of their spiritual ancestry, their spiritual ecology. This is what we have forgotten in Western civilization.

Therefore, they are the best conservationists to manage and conserve the forests and last great wildernesses as their immediate survival depends on the land and they are attuned to the environment around them, because of this, they are also the most vulnerable when it comes to ecocide, their cultures and survival is ultimately threatened. There are indigenous conservation treaty recommendations supported by many Indian and Alaska Native organizations. A recent convention set up by the Indigenous peoples of all the Americas allowed them to form sixteen principles for building a sustainable and harmonious world community.

This emerged from a 40-year-long process of reflection, consultation and action within Indigenous communities across the Americas. These principles are rooted in the concerns of hundreds of Indigenous Elders, Spiritual Leaders and Community Members, they are also rooted in deep ecology values, they recognize the interconnectedness of all life on Earth and how we affect one another and the Earth with our actions, they recognize how humans must work on internal balance to create external balance and a sustainable world, they recognize the importance of morals, and ethics in communities. These guiding principles constitute the foundation for the process of healing and developing ourselves (mentally, emotionally, physically, and spiritually), our human relationships (personal, social, political, economic, and cultural) and our relationship with Mother Earth.

The senseless annihilation of the Earth's last Rainforest which is part of preventing a vital equilibrium for the climate, has to stop along with the global unfolding ecocide of other ancient wildernesses where our great indigenous people remain.

All this destruction is for a non-renewable fuel valued over human life and all life on planet Earth. How many of us have to suffer and to what limit of destruction will this planet be pushed to, before we realize human consciousness is now an ecological issue?

We need to understand as Indigenous people already do, the roots of ecology and that we are all connected, when we hurt our environment, we destroy humanity, we are only beginning to scratch the surface of the true meaning of awakening to the illusion of our separation from nature and the universe. Despite the failure of Correa's promise of the Yasuni ITT Initiative to keep the oil in the ground, is it really a matter of requiring billions of dollars in order to do so? Are there other ways to facilitate international protection of the Ecuadorian Amazon and why are we still dependent on such a primitive source of energy extraction when we have advanced in so many other fields of technology?

The general public is accustomed to environmental and humanitarian campaigning responsibilities being the normal duty of all non-profit organisations and charities. Perhaps the reasons why we have charities and non-profits are evidence that we are living in a dysfunctional society with dysfunctional values that are out of balance with the Earth. Charities and foundations are filling a niche that the governments prefer to overlook in the name of profit and power, a niche that reflects the empty space where the rights of nature are values that do not exist in modern society, yet if we are to persist, then we must acknowledge these values and incorporate them into modern business, politics and economics. Political management of environmental resources desperately needs to become transparent or even the domain of public decision making. Since our current governments are being governed by corporations with more power than politicians and therefore they are failing to fulfil the role of environmental custodians for the rest of us. Open source software technology could create this type of transparency and public involvement in decisions on new bills and reforming laws.

Perhaps each of us has more responsibility regarding our unnecessary reliance on oil; each of us would feel this if we all knew the bigger picture. For example, not many know that the earliest cars were in fact built to process hemp bio fuel in their engines. In the 1930's Hemp Bio fuel was to be used instead of oil as a fuel for Ford's cars, this is one of the reasons among many why Cannabis is Illegal, for the sole purpose of corporations and banks in the 1930s to make millions from oil and oil by-products.

In the 1930s, Ford opened a plant in Michigan where they successfully experimented with biomass fuel conversion, proving that hemp could be used as an alternative to fossil fuels. They extracted methanol, charcoal fuel, tar, pitch ethyl-acetate, and creosote all from hemp. What this meant for Ford was that he could now not only produce their own raw materials to make cars, but he could make the fuel to run them as well. The discovery was horrible news for a man by the name of Andrew Melon, whom owned the sixth largest bank at that time in addition to much of the Gulf Oil Corporation; a company which had just recently opened their first drive-through filling station. Melon and DuPont teamed up to create a propaganda campaign to make hemp and all its material paper, fabric, crops, building materials, proteins, rope, fuel and medicine production illegal - Zach Reichard.

This is just one example which illustrates clearly that from the outset of early car manufacturing, the economic foundations of the most powerful countries was consciously based on oil, any other products that threatened investors and stakeholders were promptly removed and this is a pattern that has continued for a century and will continue unless we, ourselves, take action to adopt a more sustainable energy usage.

When you learn about some of the solutions available to mankind, one sees it is as even more of an insanity that drives oil companies and government agreements to destroy the last of the Amazon Rainforest.

You may think that all this does not affect you, everything from politics to economy is based on oil, our whole way of life is based on oil, if you are buying imported food or products from a store or supermarket or using public transport or your own car to go to work or school, you are still fuelling the destruction. Whether you like it or not, each of us is responsible, even if we see it as involuntarily responsibility, the environment is each of our responsibility, yet the majority of people think of themselves and a world separate to the natural world that they live in and are ecologically affected by, this is what can be described as a biophobic mode of thinking, a person whom is psychologically removed from nature and is almost afraid of the natural world, they have forgotten about the bigger ecological picture and how they are part of it. The earth is silently perishing as a result of our paradoxical biophobic world; this indicates that if we continue to ignore nature and our negative impact on natural ecosystems and species, we shall inevitably cause a faster degeneration of the planet.

We must start making an effort to accommodate a more ecologically-based approach to everything from industrial business, agriculture, economics, and politics to food production and sustainable architecture. We could create a sustainable economy and a fruitful one if we gave value to invisible natural capital, such as oxygen and water generation, pollination, photosynthesis and biodiversity, we would then have a better chance of survival and the Earth has a good chance of recovering from the current damage. In 2014, Petro Amazonas, a national oil Company was responsible for one of the largest terrestrial oil spills since the Texaco-Chevron case, just after drilling was permitted in Yasuni ITT national bio reserve. Over 600,000 barrels of crude oil have contaminated several rivers in the Amazon, rivers that four indigenous tribes depend upon for fishing, bathing and drinking. Some of these communities have not yet fully recovered from the Chevron oil spill twenty years ago. Now, the crude oil has reached Cuyabeno Wildlife Reserve and three weeks later, no action was taken by the Ecuadorian environmental ministry, so the impact worsened

Despite its tainted history with oil, Ecuador has not learned its lesson and for the last few years the government has opened about 800 thousand acres of Amazon rainforest in Yasuni National Park to further oil activity. Chevron saved money by intentionally bypassing environmental risk protocols which would have been the normal legal procedure if they were drilling in the USA. In the process they destroyed the area of the Ecuadorian rainforest affecting five indigenous tribes and polluting their ancestral land and rivers with billions of gallons of oil and waste water over a number of years, waste that went into the Amazon Rivers and land surface, instead of pumping it back underground. These methods are deemed substandard and toxic to human and environmental health around the world. Oil exploitation, is supposedly in the name of 'development', yet this need is really driven by Ecuador's growing debt of around 10 billion dollars owed to China, that is about nineteen percent of Ecuador's GDP. Over 520,000 barrels per day (bpd) is exported to China, although it is estimated that only about 15,000 bpd actually go directly to China, the rest of that oil is traded onwards to other countries by China. The rest of Ecuador's Oil goes to the USA. According to the oil scientists, there is barely more than twenty years' worth of oil left below the soil in Ecuador, and it is not the finest quality either.

However, if Ecuador does not take steps to find sustainable alternatives, the economy is doomed to collapse when the oil runs out and the ecological consequences on the Amazon and its indigenous populations are genocidal and ecocidal. More than ever before, the situation in Ecuador should sound alarm bells with issues such as world debt, violation of indigenous people's land rights and the root addiction to petroleum driving rapid environmental destruction through biased short-sightedness. These are all factors that could be learned from, to create a more sustainable global ecological economy in the future. When we do eventually move to sustainable alternatives from an oil-based economy, we will start to see strength in the global economy emerge; if the global economy continues to stay based on oil, all we have left for its future IA environmental destruction and an unsustainable doomed future. We could also see the economy strengthen and become less volatile if we put a value on ecosystems goods and services; this is explored in further chapters on the Ecological Economy.

Everything, even finances, depends on ecology and maintaining healthy ecosystems. On a positive note, we are seeing an exciting boom in sustainable and alternative technologies available today with advances in 3D printing, solar technologies and other alternative energy systems. Technologies which Ecuador and other countries dealing with the same problems could use and that would allow the Amazon rain forest to stay intact. However, these solutions continue to go ignored while the interest of decision makers, are money motivated rather than ecologically motivated. In 2008, Ecuador became the first country to include Rights for Nature in its Constitution, however this has been completely ignored and despite the attempts of an Ecuadorian environmental group called Yasunidos.org and international environmental activists uniting to request a referendum in 2014, the result was that the Ecuadorian government denied the request after tampering and destroying 800,000 signature petitions that were collected, the international request was simply ignored and drilling commenced earlier in June 2014, in Yasuni National Park.

President Correa made false promises several years ago to keep the oil in the ground for an impossible sum of money from the international community, however the Ecuadorian government had at the same time promised China access to oil under Yasuni national park. Indigenous groups in Ecuador have been recognised under the United Nations to which there exists a non-binding agreement, which gives indigenous groups the chance to defend their lives, land, and culture. [8]Guaranteed throughout the Declaration is the right to a process of "Free, Prior and Informed Consent" for indigenous peoples when faced with decisions, projects, or legislation by corporations or government that may affect their people and/or territory. Article 57, point 7 of the 2008 Constitution of Ecuador guarantees free, prior and informed consultation, within a reasonable period; however, this does not require consent (and is not binding). Article 82 refers explicitly to environmental consultation, in the case of a state decision which might affect the environment, and specifies broad and timely information for those affected. However, even if there is a majority opposing the project in question, it may still be carried out on the condition that the impact on those affected and the ecosystem is minimised.

It has only been a short time since that drilling has commenced in Yasuni bio reserve and already we are looking at large-scale irreversible ecocide, which is likely to get far worse if the international communities do not intervene now. To add further concern to this horror, there are several un-contacted tribes in Yasuni national park that are extremely vulnerable to disease upon contact and traumatic displacement upon invasion of their territories by oil companies, which constitutes genocidal consequences for them. Oil scientists have estimated that there is only twenty years supply of oil left under the ground in Ecuador. Therefore, we need to be looking at sustainable solutions in place of short-term gain that will create long-term impact of environmental devastation and possible economic collapse when the oil has gone.

Following Ecuadorian protests and successful campaigns to raise awareness of the threats to Yasuni bio reserve, on the fourth of December 2013, the Pacha Mama Alliance's sister foundation in their Ecuador office was illegally dissolved by government officials, the reasons were never clearly defined and legal battles still ensue over this. It is possible that this was not just because the Government wanted to remove a high profile organisation considered to be an obstacle to Correa's oil exploitation plans of Yasuni bio reserve, but also to remove the possibility of alternative sustainable transport technologies entering the Amazon that would have radically changed life for the indigenous communities that rely on navigating the Amazon rivers.

The Pacha Mama foundation was collaborating with high profile foreign organisations which were funding a solar canoe project which could have provided sustainable public transport for the Achuar community. Many of the indigenous rely on buying petrol to power motors to navigate between their communities on the Amazon Rivers between Ecuador and Peru, to hunt and to fish. Solar powered canoes would have given the Indigenous communities further independence from relying on needing money to buy petrol for travelling on the Amazon Rivers with petrol-motor powered canoes. Governments worldwide already dislike indigenous people for their self-sufficiency and their knowledge of plant medicine. These self-reliant indigenous communities are seen as a threat to the capitalist machine and to the oil industries globally which is why they and any organisation or individuals that help them, suffer constant persecution.

Meanwhile, early in 2015 the [9]Colombian government has launched a pioneering and promising ground breaking initiative to protect biodiversity and the future of the Amazon Rainforest, to create the world's largest Ecological wildlife corridor which spans over an area of 135 million hectares (1.35m km^2), According to Colombia's President Juan Manuel Santos, the protected area will be located in Brazilian and Colombian territory, with 62% of the reserve in Brazil and 34% in Colombia, and 4% in southern Venezuela. It has been dubbed the "Triple-A corridor", due to the fact that its determined area would take in a significant quota of the Andean, Amazonian and Atlantic regions of northern South America. The Triple-A corridor was the concept of Martín von Hildebrand, the director of the Amazon branch of the global environmental NGO Gaia Foundation. Ideally if NGOs and environmental campaigners pushed to get Ecuador and Peru to join this initiative, we could still have a chance of saving a significant area of the South Western area of the Amazon Basin.

There is a large movement of Environmental scientists, law makers and campaigners who have dedicated their lives to protecting the environment and ecosystems such as the Amazon. These environmental campaigners are fighting for the rights of equality for all on a political level and ecological level, so more rights are being given to Mother Earth, and all people including indigenous people involved in pressuring governments and lawmakers to acknowledge ecocide as a threat to humanity and peace, therefore it is in international interest and responsibility to make ecocide a crime. There is a world campaign against these out-dated corrupt quasi-democratic political systems worldwide. We need transparency in all government systems, so the core political stakeholders stop making billions from destroying the planet.

Globally, there is a deep level of corruption to be concerned about in the Petroleum industry; one oil company can make billions of profit in a single hour. [10] Deutsche Bank revealed in a recent report comparing British BP with Shell Oil profits that a company like British Petrol makes, on average, over US $60 billion per quarter, divide by 90 days in a quarter and 24 hours per day, gives an hourly profit rate of 30 to 50 million US dollars **per hour**. When an oil company and its financial stakeholders in government have such earning power do you really think they are going to give it all up to let humanity and the planet Earth have cleaner energy? Such profit capabilities creates a monster power that is fiercely guarded, which reflects in global policies changing, as many key political decision makers are big stakeholders of the oil industry. This will continue until such decision makers are replaced with environmental conservationists and ecologists that are motivated to keep humanity sustainable.

If we had tougher international laws that made ecocide a crime against humanity and for the protection of the Earths key ecosystems that encourage a deeper respect for natural resources worldwide. It is clear that in the current crisis limitations must be placed on what corporations get away with in terms of environmental exploitation. We especially need to be concerned with bringing these implementations to multi-national corporations that are the new politicians and presidents. For example, in the USA, the 113th Congress wrote vast quantities of legislation and took votes that are so far beyond being environmentally damaging, that it has earned the title of "most anti-environmental" body in history. According to [11]Sierra Club's *Polluting Democracy* report "The returns which big polluters are getting on these political investments -- in the form of billions in corporate tax hand-outs -- exceed 5000 percent, demonstrating that Congress remains the best "investment" possible for the coal, oil, and gas industries. The US Supreme Court opened the floodgates for a tidal wave of corrupting political cash in 2010, when the disastrous ruling in Citizens United v. FEC let a handful of big money campaign donors spend unlimited amounts of outside dollars in 'lobbying' to influence elections. How is this democratic? "What if an investment advisor told you that he could get you $59 back for every $1 you gave him? That's a 5800 percent rate of return. If you're the oil, gas, and coal industry, it's legal and business as usual in Washington. This is a legal scamming system and nowhere near a democracy, if money is used in this way to manipulate political decisions which completely negate environmental legislations and environmental protection.

'The USA 2012 election is known as most expensive election in history. The estimated $6 billion spent during the election cycle included massive contributions from some of the nation's biggest polluters, including the Koch Brothers, a pair of Kansas billionaires deeply entrenched in the oil refining, pipeline, coal, chemical, and gas sectors. According to an Oil Change International analysis, the industry spent over 70 million dollars on the 113th Congress cycle on campaign contributions and lobbying in Washington D.C. "
Sierra Club Report.

Since then, the political system has become a polluter playground and this is not just in the USA, it is worldwide.

What will the rest of us that care do about this, what will you or I do to take action? We will not remain calm and buy more petrol for our cars, we will demonstrate, write letters to advocacy websites, newspapers, petition government departments, make presentations at schools and universities, some of us will stand in the path of soldiers, their guns, bulldozers and oil inspectors. We will take to the streets, we can be heard and seen on the radio and television of the people's media, we will run our own news campaigns; we will inform and teach our children on the importance of sustainable and renewable energy resources so as not to make the same mistakes. We will build communities and workshops on sustainable energy solutions to raise awareness, we will continue to resist until the rainforest and its people are safe and gain as much support as needed, and some of us might give our lives to protect the rainforest. Everything we do, no matter how large or small, each of our efforts is valuable energy that can build towards positive change, this is the only way to create new parameters for a more sustainable world for the planet and therefore for humanity. We are empowered, we are the majority, we choose what to consume, grow, build, read, write and create, therefore we have more power than unethical political decision makers or corporations have. People, who care, are growing tired of seeing corporations have more rights than human beings or for that matter more rights than planet Earth. Earth deserves to be valued a lot higher than we do and to be protected internationally with a treaty that focuses on valuing Earth for the life which she gives us and protecting her from ecocide for the same reason.

At the time this book went to press, the Chinese government announced plans to build a 5,000 km railway from Chile to Brazil which will rip through the Amazon jungle in Peru, Ecuador and Brazil, through previously undisturbed indigenous territory of various uncontacted tribes, this will not only decimate these tribes but it will also increase the already rapid destruction of the Amazon, as it will speed up the extraction of oil, minerals and hardwoods from these areas to the outside world, increasing biodiversity loss and fragmentation. This is one of the worst possible projects that could happen to the Amazon rainforest at a time it needs more emphasis on conservation than development.

ENDNOTES: Chapter 3.

1. J.Freeman 1997. Map of Pipelines in Ecuador

2. Convention on Biological Diversity http://www.cbd.int/convention/

3. Mark Plotkin. (1993) *Tales of a Shaman's Apprentice*. Viking

a) Downloadable Report- Paul Sabin, (1967-1993) *Searching for Middle Ground. Native Communities in Northern and Central Amazon in Ecuador*

b) Downloadable Report- Oil Watch (2006) *The Right Hand of the Empire*

c) Downloadable Report-Judith Kimerly. (3rd Nov, 2006) *Indigenous Peoples and the Oil Frontier in Amazonia: The Case of Ecuador.*

4. Brian O' Leary, (1 Nov. 2008) *The Energy Solution Revolution.* Bridger House Publishers

5. Carlita Shaw (Oct 2013). *Ecocide in Ecuador*. The Ecologist. http://www.theecologist.org/blogs_and_comments/Blogs/2134611/ecocide_in_ecuador.html

6. Four Worlds International-*Sixteen Principles for building a Sustainable and Harmonious World-* http://www.fwii.net

7. Downloadable Report -Sierra Club (2014) *Polluting our Democracy and our Environment.* March

8. Article 57. Ecuador Constitution http://www.foresttransparency.info/ecuador/2012/themes/17/115/

9. Triple Corridor Initiative- Giles Constantine (February, 2015) *Colombia Heads Plan to Create 'Ecological Corridor' and Establish The World's Largest Protected Area*. Eye on Latin America-. https://eyeonlatinamerica.wordpress.com/2015/02/23/colombia-ecological-corridor/

10. Comparing British BP with Shell Oil profits-
http://www.iii.co.uk/articles/182699/shell-vs-bp-who-wins

Chapter 4: We are not Protesters but Protectors.

"*The measure of a free society is not how it treats its good citizens, but how it treats its dissidents.*" - Glenn Greenwald

It started way back when Margret Thatcher was still in power, I remember seeing and hearing the words that the politicians and media came up with ''Environmental Terrorists'', a label for environmental campaigners, animal rights activists and conservationists that were now being seen as a threat to everyone that wanted to make money, a media campaign was swiftly implemented to make people forget that we are not protesters but protectors of the environment.

In the mid-1980s, these corporations got together and created a new word "eco-terrorist" because at the time, these protest movements were growing very quickly and effectively, and they had widespread public support. There clearly was a concern that unless public opinion shifted, there'd be a really big problem on their hands". – [1]Will Potter, 'Green is the New Red'.

What Will Potter does is bring people's attention to the new speak and rhetoric that has been carefully used by politicians and their media vehicles for social engineering. [2] Whistle-blowers and journalists can now risk imprisonment for speaking out, this was new legislation implemented in 2014, the very fact this has become a political measure indicates that we definitely do not live in a democracy. While any hope for improved transparency in governments globally is becoming less apparent, it is more like a global movement where special intelligence agencies, politicians, banks and corporations enjoy further protection and privacy as a result of new laws enforced to discourage any form of investigative journalism which has been valued in the past by people such as Edward Snowdon and Julian Assand to expose corruption, while we see our privacy and human rights further eroded. We really need to be campaigning for further transparency on these government agencies that are not wholly operating for the good of all, this is clearly evident. The "war on terrorism" allows governments to treat everyone as an equally suspected terrorist, not just international, however domestic terrorists are now seen as equally threatening to governments, they are usually local activists involved in some form of campaign or advocacy work, including Greenpeace campaigners, environmentalists and journalists. If you are caught handing out leaflets perhaps to raise awareness of pollution in your local community, you could be accused of inciting terrorism.

2014 was a good year for law reformers and politicians pulling the reigns in on free speech, in a meeting with the United Nations, [3]David Cameron stated that people campaigning for the truth into the September 911 attacks on the World Trade Centre and conspiracy theorists were to be considered in the same league as the ISIL challenge as threats to society and labelled non-violent extremists. [4]Peter Drew from The Centre of Research on Globalisation, submitted an open letter to David Cameron in response to his speech asking Mr Cameron if he was aware of many members of US Congress demanding that President Obama release the 28 redacted pages of the 9/11 Commission Report, because there is information in those pages that will shock the nation, according to the two members of Congress who have been authorised to view the pages?

Or, if Mr Cameron was aware that more than the dozens of first-responder fire fighters who risked their lives on 9/11 and who lost 343 of their colleagues that day, including those who formed the organisation '*Fire Fighters for 9/11 Truth*' and that more than 2,200 professional architects, engineers, and demolition experts from the organisation '*Architects & Engineers for 9/11 Truth*' in addition to 100,000 New York residents signed a petition calling for a new investigation into the collapse of World Trade Centre Building 7 through the '*High Rise Safety Initiative*'?''

Hasn't this 'war on terrorism' greatly benefited governments and corporations alike to tighten the belt of their gain for more control and power over the average people and their freedom of speech, thought and expression - people who are simply trying to make the world a better place? There are the rare extreme cases of animal activists or environmental activists damaging property in certain situations, but these are not common. For the most part, environmental conservation and campaigning has, and continues to be, a peaceful work carried out by normal people, but which has now become dangerous work due to their being labelled "non-violent extremists, eco-terrorists, environmental terrorists, and conspiracy theorists", while governments continue to encourage discrimination and condemnation of environmentalists, human and animal rights campaigners, journalists and whistle-blowers, as a threat to society, all in the same league of extreme terrorism.

Now these reforming laws that are chipping away at human rights and allowing the governments to spy on people are also progressing towards fascism that is becoming systematic in its rise from country to country. This includes internet-gagging and cyber-gagging laws in the name of anti-terrorism or to 'protect copyright' content which are really used to block or control the free flow of information or access to websites that are for researchers, journalism, environmental activism, truth and justice. This is a form of socially engineered persecution to protect the elite, corporate giants and prominent politicians from being further exposed. While our pursuit towards truth, justice, and defending the natural environment against exploitation is becoming a dangerous pursuit more to us and our liberty than to the elite and their corporate investments. Environmental and animal-rights activists are now considered the United States' number-one domestic terrorism threat, and they can now be prosecuted as criminals and go to jail.

''Environmentalists question at the core, what it is to be a human being, we ask to re-evaluate the whole economic system, how we produce our food, our clothing, industry and transportation, and there is a lot of vested political interest in all of those things'' – Will Potter

Due to this progressive persecution of any form of activism for truth and justice, there is an increase in the murders of environmental and truth defenders, as now laws and selected judges seem to be more in favour of politicians and their corporate investments rather than truth and justice, which becomes a subconscious affirmation, making it easier for those that do the killing to literally get away with murder.

Let us look at some very recent examples:

In May 2013, [5]Jairo Mora Sandoval, a Sea Turtle Conservationist was found naked beaten and murdered on a beach after being dragged behind a car. The seven defendants allegedly from a well-known poaching gang were put on trial till several years later and due to lost and botched evidence, they walked free from the court room.

On the 1st of September 2014, [6]Edwin Chota, a prominent Peruvian anti-logging activist was shot dead along with three of his colleagues in front of other villages by illegal loggers. He had previously asked the authorities for protection following death threats, he had dedicated his life to defending the ancestral land of the Alto Tamaya-Saweto community to gain titles to their land and defend them against illegal loggers. He had previously given interviews with National Geographic and the New York Times. Despite his pleas for protection the authorities did nothing to help.

Here in Ecuador in December 2014, just before the Peru Climate talks were to take place, a Shuar environmental activist called [7]José Tendetza was bound up by rope, tortured, murdered and dumped in a river, he was planning on going to the Peru climate talks at the beginning of December to discuss the mining oil exploitation in his community by a Chinese Mining company EcuaCorrientes, though it is suspected officials were involved. The Yasunidos activist group, were also stopped by government officials from going to the Peru Climate talks in their bus, the vehicle was confiscated by police and they were arrested on false claims that they did not have the right papers to drive the vehicle. In Peru more activists were murdered just before the talks, at least 57 activists had been killed in Peru and more than 60 percent of them murdered in the last few years.

The deaths or persecution of environmentalists has been increasing rapidly over the last 5 years, especially in Latin and Central America where more than 80 percent of deaths of environmental defenders are reported according to a survey done by [8]*Global Witness*. Brazil, is the world's worst country for environmental defenders being killed with 448 deaths between 2002 and 2013, all of those are indigenous people defending their land against dam building, oil, mining or deforestation.

''Never has it been more important to protect the environment, and never has doing that been more deadly. Competition for access to natural resources is intensifying against a backdrop of extreme global inequality, while humanity has already crossed several vital planetary environmental boundaries. At the same time, more and more ordinary people are finding themselves on the frontline of the battle to defend their environment from corporate or state abuse, and from unsustainable exploitation. This rapidly worsening crisis appears to be hidden in plain sight. A lack of systematic monitoring or awareness of the growing threat to environmental and land activists is enabling killings and a wide range of other abuses, while national governments and judicial systems are regularly failing to protect their citizens from harm.'' - Global Witness-Deadly Environment Report

Despite this deteriorating situation, there are some positive measures being taken by concerned and prominent people in environmental and the human rights sector. There have been several tribunals organised by a group defending the Rights of Nature, the second tribunal for the Rights of Nature was held in Peru in 2014, thirteen distinguished judges heard twelve prominent cases, The Tribunal proceedings were intense and deeply moving as witness after witness gave intimate testimony reinforced by scientific evidence of experts. Indigenous activists such as Casey Camp-Horinek, Ponca Nation, USA and Patricia Gualinga, Sarayaku, were all representing environmental threats to their communities and discussed Indigenous cosmo-vision to lay the foundation for understanding Mother Earth and living in harmony with nature.

Although the tribunal does not have direct legal authority its aim is *''to provide a framework for educating civil society and governments on the fundamental tenets of Rights of Nature and an instrument for legal experts to examine constructs needed to more fully integrate Rights of Nature.''*

Polly Higgins is a UK based lawyer whom has dedicated her life's work to making Ecocide an acknowledgeable international crime, like genocide. She submitted a draft of the law in 2010. She brings public attention to the Rome Statute, a statute of countries that make up an International Criminal Court with the aim for a peace treaty against genocide, human rights violations and ecocide was on the list until it was removed in 1996. However, thanks to the work of Polly Higgins and her campaign to add Ecocide back to the Rome Statute to make it the 5th crime against peace, we hope this can be achieved, the more people that are aware of this possibility, the more people can support and push for it to become a reality.

ENDNOTES: Chapter 4.

1. Will Potter. 'Green is the New Red'

2. Paul Farrell (26th September, 2014) *Journalists and whistleblowers will go to jail under new national security laws*. The Guardian News.

3. David Cameron Speech at the UN (September, 2014) *Non Violent Conspiracy Theorists and Whistle-blowers are Just As Dangerous as ISIS*

4. Peter Drew Open Letter to David Cameron. The Centre of Research on Globalisation, you can find it online.

5. Jeremy Hance (Jan, 27, 2015) Suspects *acquitted in shocking murder of sea turtle conservationist.*

6. Scott Wallace (Sept, 2014) Quadruple *Homicide in Peruvian Amazon Puts Criminal Logging in Spotlight.* National Geographic.

7. Juan Falconi Puig (December, 2014) *Ecuador has set up independent inquiry into the death of the indigenous leader José Tendetza.*

8. Global Witness Press release (Jan 1st 2014) Deadly *Environment Report.* globalwitness.org

Chapter 5: Ecological Economy

"*To reverse the effects of civilisation would destroy the dreams of a lot of people. There's no way around it. We can talk all we want about sustainability, but there's a sense in which it doesn't matter that these people's dreams are based on, embedded in, intertwined with, and formed by an inherently destructive economic and social system. Their dreams are still their dreams. What right do I -- or does anyone else -- have to destroy them. At the same time, what right do they have to destroy the world?"* — Derrick Jensen, Endgame, Vol. 1: The Problem of Civilisation

The word 'economy' is defined by how communities of people choose to use their environmental resources to meet their chosen living requirements, therefore economy, should have always been based on ecological principles to begin with. Human life depends on goods and services provided by nature, therefore, it is our duty to manage what we utilise from Earth sustainably, if we want to keep the Earth Bank sustainable, we must invest in its future and its present invisible production of goods and services. We can explore innovative strategies to transfer an entire economy built on principles within the Earth's ecological carrying capacity, (within the limitations of the Earth's natural resources). When our current economy is based on oil, this can only mean ecological destruction, as it is the only way to gain profit and improve the economy as it is, if we transferred our economy from this destructive pattern, to be based on ecological values in terms of financial capital, we would not only secure life on Earth to prosper but our economy will be sustainable and evolve in unexpected ways.

We have an oil-based economy, most of the world believes that oil comes from fossil fuels and is in limited supply which allows oil prices to soar in the USA, destabilising the economy and there are those that believe oil to come from abiotic sources. With this dichotomy aside, we still have too many roads and cars and although we have the technology for alternative fuels and energies, the oligarchs will not lessen their grip from oil, which is causing much of the global ecocidal destruction.

The current world economic collapse being experienced in developed countries is a sign that we need to re-evaluate an economy that has been built on short-term gain and with no acknowledgement or regard for nature's capital, invisible goods, services and production. This complete disregard to nature's capital is so engrained in our perception of the world. We could start exploring new ways of seeing nature as an investment to preserve biodiversity and the natural balance of ecosystems for the future of humanity. Every living species of plant and animal and ecosystem has a role in nature's bio-production which has financial value in natural capital. This is a very exciting concept that could revolutionise, reshape and immediately shift a destructive debt ridden oil based economy to an entirely sustainable and wealthy one. However, just like other similar solutions to humanities problems, it may be difficult to implement an economy based on Natural Capital, as it may pose as a threat and may not be adopted by the elite 1 percent, whom wish to maintain their power and control over centralized management of the world's natural resources and maintaining world debt is a way to do this. The most powerful companies in the oil, chemical and biopharmaceutical industries also would have to pay the largest costs for environmental damage to natural capital, through negligence of Corporate Social Responsibility (CSR), to the environment and severe damage to ecosystems. The environment needs to be a larger priority for Corporate Social Responsibility.

[1]'The Green Economy Initiative' of the United Nations Environment Programme, (UNEP) and other efforts are now underway to improve the way in which we value and account for nature in our economic decision-making, a new foundation for switching to an ecological economy and putting value on ecosystems and natural capital. Recent initiatives, such as the global study on

[2]'The Economics of Ecosystems and Biodiversity' (TEEB), has resulted in a better understanding of the economic value of forests and other ecosystems for societies, as an example. The TEEB study estimates that the world's national parks and protected areas generate wealth via nature-based goods and services equal to around US $5 trillion per year in terms of biodiversity value.

Ecosystems provide us with food, clean air and water, while forests provide protection from soil erosion, recreational services, medicinal products, and climate regulation. The *World Resource Institute* (WRI) estimates the value of ecosystem services to be US $33 trillion a year, nearly twice the value of the global gross national product (GNP) of US $18 trillion. The US is also in debt by 17 trillion dollars, if the US switched to an economy based on natural capital, it would take care of this debt.

In the same way that a banknote is a promissory note against the gold or silver that has been deposited in the bank, ecological economists are seeing how we can start to put the same value onto ecosystems and the role of species in ecosystem production, another example, would be the 80 percent of oxygen produced by algae in the ocean. Hypothetically, the value of ecosystems that exist could regenerate local economies and increase the wealth and monetary value of nature globally, simply by ensuring its conservation and existence by using initiatives similar to the TEEB.

Nature's ecological banking system could be a way to revolutionise our world and local economies and transfer wealth from an oil-based economy to an ecology-based economy, this wealth would provide poor countries with enough ecological economy that global debt would become a thing of the past. This starts on a local level worldwide, which would regenerate and allow local communities to have better control over their own natural resources, protecting and managing them from over-exploitation of previously decentralised management of resources, which could be prevented, if corporate social responsibility pays a tax to the natural capital destroyed and when more is taken out of the ecosystems and Natural Capital, than is put into them, this crucially needs to be taken into account in order to gain more balance. This form of converting nature into capital would boost the world economy, as well as local economies on so many levels; it would also provide millions of new jobs and professions for ecological accountants, auditors and bookkeepers.

[3]Pavan Sukhdev was involved in setting up the TEEB initiative and he says that "*the stuff of life is natural capital*", he proposed putting a value on natural capital in order to ensure its conservation, he says

that there is an abundance of unclaimed financial goods in ecosystem services that would breathe life into the poorest communities, they are important benefits of public wealth, and it is usually the poorest people that manage these ecosystems. Payment for Ecosystem Services (PES) are agreements whereby a user of an ecosystem service makes a payment to an individual or communities whose practices such as land use or deforestation directly affects the use of that ecosystem services. Pavan, points out that when we measure our GDP, we don't include our biggest assets at the country level at the local level, which would be the Natural Capital of each country. When we measure Corporate Social Responsibility we do not consider our impacts or costs on nature, or human health or society, and that needs to stop, '*You cannot manage what you do not measure"* - Pavan Sukhdev.

A community at a local geographic level, as well as at a global level, has the power to change the direction of humanity, so perhaps while governments continue to ignore the crisis, we in our local communities can start taking action to change things at this level, and we can start Nature Capital initiatives in local communities and councils. Sustainability empowers the planet and people; this is the only route for humanity to take if it is to stop species extinction and to have a chance of survival. We have to invest in sustainability by also investing more in conservation and designing an ecological economy, an entirely new economy built on the principles within the Earth's natural carrying capacity, which means that we make economic decisions according to the limitations of our ecological natural resources. This would be an investment in both nature and ourselves.

If only governments would invest in conserving natural resources and wildlife conservation as they do in the world banking systems, after all, planet Earth is the bank of life, only when we begin to see this, will things change, when the value of all life on Earth is seen as an ecological asset that helps keep the planet functioning in balance. While these important ecological values are being ignored, species extinction and ecocide will continue till we have no choices left. There is still a seed of hope for a shift in human consciousness from a political-economic hierarchical pyramid structure to a more sustainable equal or holographic way of operating politically, socially and economically through improved transparency in governments and financial institutions and an ecologically sustainable economy, where all humans have an equal chance at wealth and quality of life. An ecological economy would allow more people to see and value nature and ecosystems, let alone, how we are interconnected to all life on Earth.

There is a great resistance for this to take place at government levels, as the addiction to power drives a great fear of the loss of power, which is also why alternative cleaner energies have been avoided, therefore we are being made to persist in this state of doomed atrophy on all levels of reality. The seeds of hope are within every one of us. We are all responsible for this crisis; it takes those of us that are courageous enough to implement these changes. Putting financial value on Natural Capital is a 'Commons' concept which would allow communities to locally maintain and manage natural capital and resources locally would also be a regenerative concept for natural economy.

"a dilemma in which multiple individuals acting independently in their own self-interest can ultimately destroy a shared resource even where it is clear that it is not in anyone's long-term interest for this to happen" – [4] Hardin. 1968 on The Tragedy of the Commons.

ENDNOTES: Chapter 5

1. United Nations Green Economy- http://www.unep.org/greeneconomy/

2. TEEB Initiative Report available online.

3. Pavan Sukhdev- Ted Talks Put a Value on Nature

4. a) Garrett Hardin (December 13, 1968) The Tragedy of the Commons. Published in Science.

b) De Young, R (1999) Tragedy of the Commons. In D. E. Alexander & R. W. Fairbridge [Eds] Encyclopaedia of

Environmental Science. (Pp. 601-602) Hingham, MA: Kluwer Academic Publishers.

Chapter 6: Water, Rain, Life.

Corporate privatisation and control of water on foreign soil has caused poor people unnecessary suffering and death. This is a matter which is beginning to affect people in developed countries, we need to explore ways which we can generate clean water such as new systems where we can suck water out of the air for clean drinking water, or simply by collecting rainwater in regions where there is plenty of rain, although this has been made illegal in some North American States.

[1]Trevor James Constable did his last public interview with me before completely retiring from the public eye to focus on refining his latest rain-engineering devices. Trevor James Constable's [2]etheric rain-engineering technologies are not to be confused with geo-engineering or chemtrails, which are a government operation using cocktails of various toxic metals and chemicals to alter the climate temperature by reflecting the sun's rays, many scientists are concerned that the substances being sprayed in a worldwide operation are currently harming human health and contaminating soil, crops, fresh water sources with toxic loads of aluminium, barium, arsenic and various other substances, it is claimed that chemtrails are used to create a plasmic field of electromagnetic nanoparticles in the atmosphere for HAARP technologies. In comparison, Trevor's etheric rain-engineering technology is an ecologically sound and clean technology using suppressed science that uses the aetheric forces to clean the air and/or make rain where there are insufficient amounts of rain. This technology can not only put an end to air pollution and clean water scarcity, it can also be used to stabilise the climate in a completely natural way. It has been used and tested in many locations from California, Los Angeles, to clean up air pollution to making rain in Malaysia after long drought, with successful collaborations with some government officials who were open to using the technology. Unfortunately, the largest barrier to this amazing work is the fact that many governments are opposed to its use. The reason for this is because most governments find it threatening to their agendas to control water, introducing this technology would mean a loss of power and money in water

management in that respect, therefore its availability, like many free energy technologies, has met with great resistance.

The last contact I had with Trevor was a few years ago after calling him and speaking to him on the phone, after hearing that he had been recovering from a number of strokes. Trevor is an incredible pioneer, who has led a fascinating life and who had the opportunity to meet and work with some other great pioneers and scientists who had less fortunate endings to their lives due to oligarchic suppression of their technologies.

Trevor James Constable is an amazing man whom has developed technologies from Wilhelm Reich's work on Aether Science, which is not acknowledged by mainstream science. So his work is virtually unheard of, yet he is responsible for chemical free, rain-making technologies for desert environments simply by using Aether science. His techniques are based on Wilhelm Reich's cloud-buster technologies and other pioneering methods that continue to be suppressed by governments. The list for sustainable technology possibilities is very extensive and it provides many exciting avenues to explore and implement.

Trevor Constable was born in 1927 in New Zealand; he emigrated to the USA in 1952 after graduating from university as an Engineer. His varied career included over thirty years as a Merchant Navy Radio Officer and his Merchant Marine Service involved more than 300 ocean crossings, he was also a Professional Pilot. During his time at sea, he worked on various devices where he learned to engineer rain without the use of chemicals or electromagnetic radiation, a technique based on devices which he built and adapted from Dr Wilhelm Reich's work. Wilhelm Reich was one of the most controversial figures of the twentieth century. Dr Reich died in a federal prison, while the American government banned his books and destroyed his research; some of his banned books have since been restored through the Wilhelm Reich Museum. Dr Reich invented a weather modification device called the cloud-buster, based on the repressed and denied science of the aether. Many versions and adaptations have been used since in different parts of the world. The cloud-buster uses no chemicals or electromagnetic radiation. It is one of the devices of future technology that acknowledges the aether, life force, or chi energy. On his own initiative, over the last sixty years, Trevor investigated further adaptations of the cloud-buster as he saw its potential advantages for humanitarian efforts. He has proved his findings with many hours of time-lapse video tape during his tests on cargo ships and as a flight pilot over sixty years. Successful airborne cloud-buster operations have been carried out in Hawaii, Malaysia and China.

Trevor also enjoyed a prestigious career in copy-writing and broadcasting. He became an expert chronicler and documenter of famous fighter planes in aviation history, his aviation books have been translated into many different languages. Trevor also published ten non-fiction books. The roots of his weather engineering work are connected with his observation in the unseen realms of UFO phenomena, on which he has written two books, one of his masterworks is his book "The Cosmic Pulse of Life" describing the revolutionary biological power behind some kinds of UFOs, originally published in 1975, this book is acknowledged for building bridges in human understanding, therefore developing human consciousness.

Formal science does not acknowledge the existence of the aether, etheric force or vital force.

Trevor found that the aetheric force which he uses in his rain engineering work is the same energy behind some of those mysterious biological objects, which we term as UFOs, there are many different kinds of UFOs, some are biological, this is a concept many find difficult to grasp, but if we can acknowledge that the human eye is limited and cannot see through the infrared and ultra-violet spectrum, we are therefore blind to some of these biological UFOs, unless we accidentally film them on an infrared camera. One of Trevor's photos below from The Cosmic Pulse of Life.

BRAVO #3

Strange, plasmatic fauna, invisible to normal human sight, cavort above the summit of Mt. Wilson, California in January 1959. The author used a Praktica FX-2 camera, exposing at f1.9 and 1/100 second, using highspeed infrared film. These organisms, according to the author, pulsate and change form when spuriously visible and account for numerous UFO reports. Compare the larger forms in this photo with those photographed by the Spanish Air Force and appearing opposite.

Biological UFOs filmed in infrared. Photographed by TJC, 1959.

Trevor was one of the first people to start intentionally doing this as part of his investigations back in 1957. Basing his research and field assumptions that UFOs are a component of an invisible level of life, this invisible factor is acknowledged in numerous radar sightings during and since WW2, that had not been visually confirmed by pilots, yet showed up on radar readings. There are numerous UFO reports where the UFOs have been seen to dematerialise or vanish under observation, similarly, UFOs have been seen to appear to materialise under clear sky conditions.

Trevor's photographic research was a simple direct approach to extend the normal visible spectrum. He used infra-red film that records that spectrum of light and has photographed many different life forms that live in this realm that we cannot see with our own unaided human eye. There exists in this atmosphere an unseen level of life which has probably existed alongside our own for more than a millennium. There are also constructs present in that same invisible realm, engineered by a mysterious etheric force. When the life forms, or 'critters', as Trevor calls them, emerge into the visible spectrum where we can see them, they are usually confused. Trevor's discovery introduces a much needed element to add to future science and to a shattering of paradigms in conventional science and the limitation of the human senses, which Trevor explains will take future humans, generations to grasp and understand. Common functioning principles involved in both UFO categories is the biological energy that animates the 'critters' as he refers to them, and propels their craft, the visitors that have engineered their crafts, have achieved technical mastery with the aetheric force, a force which conventional science continues to deny. However, for Trevor James Constable, his investigation and understanding of these biological UFOs gave him a greater understanding of the aether and rain-engineering.

This understanding of etheric rain-engineering could eventually lead to providing access to billions of tons of water through understanding how the aetheric forces work and how to engineer them. The curse of drought can be ended for all humanity, however this is not a gift that the oligarchy wish to grant humanity, it may be a surprise to learn that they benefit from the lack of water and people starving or dying of thirst, they benefit from the concept of lack altogether. They aim to control the world's water resources, forcing high water prices on desperate and depressed people.

Trevor explains that the airborne version or P-Gun is simple technology, before any elite sponsored scientists aim to squash such claims as bizarre; I invite you to read the interview and visit the resources in the Endnotes, before coming to any conclusions. It is important to bear in mind what NASA's countless billions in expenditure have done and unwittingly verified that Trevor's original approach to studying these biological UFOs was correct. On a private research budget of fewer than two hundred dollars a month, he was ridiculed back in the 1950s, especially on his claims that these biological UFOs were from an invisible domain and appear to us only sporadically. In 1996 NASA launched its STS 75 using the Columbia Shuttle 300 miles up into space. A satellite attached to the shuttle by a special powered generating cable called a tether, the tether broke loose and drifted off more than 70 miles astern of the orbiting Colombia, the entire sequence was recorded by an ultra-violet video camera fixed to the shuttle that was broadcasting what it was filming back to ground control, who were witness to seeing dozens of luminous UFOs resembling giant jellyfish or sperm-like creatures, all swimming around the tether. Mission control asked the astronauts to describe what they could see, and it was clear they were seeing a very different situation, as they themselves did not possess ultra-violet eyesight, the astronauts could only report that the tether had broken free and was floating around 70 miles astern of the ship. Whereas ground control had a totally different perspective through the view of the ultraviolet world being recorded via the space shuttle's camera, this entire astounding sequence is available in the public domain on the internet, you can Google the famous tether incident and you will see it on YouTube. These biological UFOs were recorded dematerialising and materialising, coming in and out of view. The ultraviolet is a harmonic relative of the infra-red, some great mysteries of Ufology, dwell in and come and go from an invisible realm of vibrations or parallel worlds. These creatures resemble the 'critters' that Trevor James Constable has filmed on the Californian high desert, they are also the same UFOs featured in NASA's photographs during the Clementine shuttle journey to the moon, those photographs should be still available on NASA's USGS Geographic website.

Jose Escamilla is another documentary film producer who has also worked with Trevor James Constable and he has researched Clementine's exploration photos of the moon which shockingly revealed to be in full colour, although the public view of the moon has always been in black and white and is still presented as such, despite having colour photography technology available, the simple reason for this is that NASA doesn't allow the public to see that the moon is actually a place which has Earth hues and colours because it reveals that there is a lot more which we do not know about, not just examples of Trevor's previously documented biological UFOs but also places where you can see green hues in Moon craters. Prior astronauts that have been to the moon such as John White, explains that the Moon has a thin atmosphere and even some simple plant life and monumental structures like Stonehenge and giant Egyptian like statue structures. The reason it is important to consider this information is because there is so much that conventional science as we know it does not explain and there are reasons for this, that serve only those in power.

For the last sixty years, Trevor James Constable has come up against severe ridicule for much of his radical work which is based on very scientific investigations that explain the physical reality of the aether. Trevor's sixty years of scientific experiments included ways to reduce air pollution over Los Angeles, California, using the P-Gun Rain-engineering device strapped to cargo ships and later to an Apache airplane or helicopter. Lengthy experimentation with aetheric vortex generating equipment, these experiments were pre-notified to official sources and acknowledged as such via official documentation. In 1990 Trevor managed Operation Clincha as a full season anti-smog operation, covering four huge states in the south coast, documented by air quality management district, the responsible authority at that time. Operation Clincher used fourteen stations employing Constable's technology. The results immediately produced an astounding 24 percent reduction in smog days in the entire season, the lowest recorded smog on record in Southern California. The Journal of Borderland Research in California published an extensive article at that time. No official body or corporate groups were interested in operational Clincher, everyone had already invested in pollution, not in its abolishment, and this is the problem that we still have today. While this technology as one example that sits on 60 years of refined tuning and experimentation, has provided official document after official document of positive results that could be used to benefit cleaning up the planet and putting an end to starvation and lack of clean water; the rest of humanity and planet Earth suffers the consequences of not being allowed to use these tried and tested technologies.

A world famous military figure General Curtis LeMay actually played a part in Operation Clincher, after testing the technology himself, he wanted to bring its attention to the US air force, his death at age 83 prior to Project Clincher's completion prevented that from happening.

In 1988, George KC Rue was responsible for providing funds for Trevor's rain-engineering operations. Since then, the two have attempted to bring government attention to this technology worldwide. Some very prominent landmark operations were held in Malaysia where great achievements were made to rid Malaysia of long term drought with their rain-engineering operations.

This is one example of an amazing well tested and successful technology that is a great gift to humanity which Trevor dedicated his life to developing. Aetheric Rain-engineering could remedy drought, air pollution and climate instability worldwide, all of humanities biggest problems dealt with in a nutshell, yet the government conveniently ignore it, because they will not relinquish their way of control and profiting from scarcity.

Trevor envisions a future civilisation which will be empowered by the aetheric force, perhaps this will be when human consciousness has crossed that bridge from the old paradigm, leaving behind the current archaic destructive control system to a new way of being in an ecologically sustainable and enlightened world on these rediscovered ancient technologies.

Interview with Trevor James Constable's interview on rain - engineering, the ability to breathe life into deserts, end starvation and water shortage world wide – March 5th 2010

C: *The other books that readers may be interested in are 'Sky Creatures' published in 1978, could you tell us a little about that book?*

Trevor: *Yes, that one was published by a woman in a New York publisher, she was determined to have it come out, she got into a loggerhead situation with the publisher who didn't want to do it and he wanted large chunks of the book deleted. It is really a truncated version of 'Cosmic Pulse of Life' and not really satisfactory from my point of view.*

C: *Could you talk about one of your earlier books, 'Spacemen friends or foe?' which was published in 1956.*

Trevor: *It was the first thing which I ever published, and it led to the issue of "They live in the S". It really was just a monograph of 'Spacemen friend or foe?', which I have forgotten about.*

C: *From the 1950s to the 1990s you devoted your work to investigation and experimentation and fine tuning of your aetheric geometrically engineered rain technology and you also investigated beyond that with infrared cameras filming biological UFOs that exist in the unseen realms that we as human beings are unable to see.*

Trevor: *That led the American government to develop a special camera that reacts to ultra-violet radiation, that would objectify the biological UFOs, they also exist in the infrared, the infrared is a harmonic of the ultraviolet. I did that back in the fifties.*

C: *And NASA used your work to develop their space camera! Going back to your aetheric rain-engineering technologies, it is quite a political and socially challenging subject.*

Trevor: *Yes, it is a very challenging subject for conventional science to deal with, it forces you to accept the existence of the aether, which* *has been put to bed by Einstein, and nobody has been wanting to look at it ever since.*

C: *Let us start by working our way from aether, now from your writing you have broken aether down into four separate parts, Warm aether, Light aether, Chemical aether and Life aether.*

Trevor: *When we deal with rain-engineering, it is the chemical ether which is the important one from that view point. Wilhelm Reich, made the chemical ether illuminate in a vacuum, making its existence evident. Up on the moon, when the astronauts got out and are walking on the moon, as they are communicating with their base. The radio on their backpacks was irradiating their aethers which were outside of their space suits; they had a blue radiance that came out around them over several feet, which makes it quite obvious there is something objective there and could be objectified under those conditions for study. I don't know if they ever looked at Wilhelm Reich's work because the government burned and destroyed Reich's scientific archives and scientific experiments to prevent anyone looking at it. What we do know is that Reich succeeded in making the aether illuminate in a vacuum tube. So, from that it goes full circle when you see the astronauts with their blue illuminated aether around them which grew stronger when they spoke, which is very interesting.*

C: *This aether is such a complex primordial substance, which all life seems to be connected too, something that is very key to why Reich's work was so radical. How did you come about Reich's work and developing his work, how did that lead you to experimenting with Rain engineering?*

Trevor: *I got interested in the unseen realm and unidentified flying objects back in the 40s and 50s, a long time ago, I was looking at everything possibly pertained to it including Dr Reich's work, which was the most comprehensive investigation that had been done, by any scientific worker. I went along with it and became acquainted with the principles that stood with it, and his daughter that was the late Eva Reich, who died recently, she guided me into his work so that I didn't go off track, which is very easy for some people to do. This is because many tend to ignore the basic work that he published* *which was "The Function of the Orgasm", that is a key book for everyone to read who wants to know about Wilhelm Reich, because everything stems from the function of the organism. That is where the root is in the whole thing. All my weather engineering work goes back to that. However, most people have issues with their own sexual processes, so no-one wants to look at that. This is why we have never been really able to market these processes for controlling the weather in the fashion that is clearly obvious, it does work, no doubt about it.*

I have a suitcase full of time-lapse tapes showing that aetheric rain-engineering works. No-one can dispute that. I could probably produce 40 or 50 CDs with all the time-lapse tape that I have here. I bought a commercial tape recorder back in the 1980s when I was on the Maui ship, I actually wore that machine out, and taking time-lapse tapes with it as it is very hard on a tape recorder to use it that way. I have the material benefit of looking at those tapes when I want to or showing them to people fit to see them or showing them to presidents and prime ministers to scare the hell out of them. When you explain that you have a system that uses neither chemicals nor electric or synthetic energy to control the weather, to make it rain, they want to get under the table or leave, it frightens them it really is something, especially among high officials.

C: *Have you had any recent enquirers for demonstrations to use it? In the handbook you sent me which is very detailed, you do specify that due to the political and social issues carried by the implications of this, that you don't give demonstrations.*

Trevor: *We don't give demonstrations to anybody. They can see the evidence from the time-lapse films there is no way that anyone could fake that. It is really a functioning of what Dr Reich called Human Armouring, like body armour that a human wears, except that it is a person who prevents themselves coming into contact with something that animates his own sexual processes, they are not able to handle that. Lots of people all over the world are suffering because of this repressed technology.*

C: *It must have taken a lot of investigative flight trials to go out and understand the aether and it's oscillation cycles around the globe.*

Trevor: *This is why they are not able to do anything with hurricanes; scientists don't understand that it is to do with the superimposition of two ether streams of cosmic energy that creates a hurricane to begin with. Dr Reich was dedicated to studying this in his lifetime and he used photographic evidence that was taken by NASA in the earlier days, and proved that is how a hurricane was created. Conventional scientists and engineers just don't want to advance into aetheric science - that is what it amounts to.*

C: *Is it also because they would have to re-evaluate what they were taught in university and what we know is accepted in science and physics, but also the power agenda that is gained from suppressing this knowledge?*

Trevor: *yes, that is right; you know that from your science degree you would have to do that. People get involved economically in existing ways of doing things and they have to be careful that they don't lose their jobs, you can understand that, you can lose your job and you carry the stigma of having that happen to you which makes you less desirable and not so welcome elsewhere, unless you run into someone like me as an employer.*

C: *With your aerial rain engineering experiments, you have two hollow tubes attached to either wings of the plane?*

Trevor: *Yes, we just use one 9 inch tube now; we don't need the two tubes any more. You don't even need to place it on the wing structure; you can have it inside the cabin of the plane now. The tubes that we use are made in Japan by a ceramics organisation there, then coated with copper and a two way mirror on the end of it and it works fine. It allows you to intercept the aether and to push the aether back and when you push it back it builds up and when it builds up it attracts moisture from the atmosphere to itself, just like a magnet and it keeps coming for some time. You are likely to do a lot of damage if you attempt this in a built up area such a city, because high voltage transformers will blow out. In the banks you have these automatic teller machines and they are affected, they can gobble up your bank cards, so we have to be very careful where we do this. The aether goes through everything, it is in everything and there is nothing you can do to insulate from it.*

C: *Have you read any of Rudolph Steiner's books?*

Trevor: *Yes, of course, another great man, Steiner put me where I am today and I studied him before I studied Reich's work.*

C: *What was it about Steiner's principles that shaped your own work?*

Trevor: *The teacher who I had back in the early days, back in the 50s, was a man named Dr Franklin Thomas, he was an optometrist and a publisher in Los Angeles, he gave me a book on Steiner and said you have to get familiar with this as this is what you need to undercurrent your further development, you won't go anywhere unless you understand Steiner or give it some attention. And that was 100 percent true; it turned out to be of great benefit to me, all my life. It also made it possible for me to understand what Wilhelm Reich's work much better because I had that background with Rudolph Steiner's work beforehand. The two works connect very well. Although Reich and Steiner never knew each other or met although they are both originally from Austria.*

Gunther Watchsmooth, was Steiner's secretary for the last twenty years of Steiner's life. The lost efforts in Gunther Watchsmooth's book is verifiable on an ocean going ship, I have a lot of time-lapse film showing this, you really cannot dispute it. In the winter time, there is a flow of aetheric force, that comes out of the northern section of the Earth and it follows towards the south. That flow can be blocked locally with shipboard equipment so that it builds up into rain while being photographed and it will come right over the ship and it has been done hundreds of times, not just once or twice.

I have an ally who is a Professor at a British University, he was responsible for encouraging my curiosity into many of these things and is now devastated, exultant by what I have done.

C: *What kind of equipment would you use on a ship? Would it be like a P-Gun? Please explain what a P-gun is.*

Trevor: *Yes, anything like that, I entrusted a P-Gun to a deputy and it made colossal problems with the weather. So unless we were specifically using it we would have to take it down or get into* *trouble. A P-Gun is an empty tube, there is nothing in the tube at all, except for mirrors in the end of it, a two-way mirror. That is the secret to making it work, the mirror reflects through the tube from the end. It empties the aether out of the tube as the aether will not go against the mirror, which is a cardinal principle of aetheric rain-engineering, that produces low potential within the tube, low potential feeds into the higher potential outside, that is the way the ether works, it flows from low potential to high potential. That is what puzzles the academics all the time.*

C: *One of the examples you used in your book was Anwar Ibrahim a man with the Malaysian government who was brave enough to try it out.*

Trevor: *Yes, Anwar Ibrahim was a great man and he will come again, he was ousted from the government by underhanded means, beaten up and tortured, he survived it all and I expect one day he would become prime minister of Malaysia, I thought he was a splendid individual because he took me right into his office and listened to what I had to say and he saw I was a straight-ahead guy and he got the bureaucracy out of the way and got us going and we made rain in Malaysia because of him.*

C: *"There were ten days of wild rain"*

Trevor: *That is right, and at night, the city of Kuala Lumpur was like it was under a bombing attack, there was tremendous lightening, that scared just about everybody, I have film of that too.*

C: *And that was after almost five months of regional drought?*

Trevor: *That is right,*

C: *It is just staggering that we are sitting on this incredible technology that you have developed, and it was back in 1991 that these trials in Malaysia were carried out and you have been working on this for a long time now, why is it that governments do not want it to be made available to humanity?*

Trevor: *The key to the whole thing is that the wealthy oligarchy individuals whom actually control the world, want world drought,* *that is a particular agenda that they follow, so they stifle every opportunity that you get to deal with drought, they will come and talk to the prime minister or president of that country and he goes down like a pricked balloon, he will not take on rain-engineering after he has talked to the oligarchs, they make sure that he loses interest or else, out he goes.*

C: *And they profit from drought?*

Trevor: *The oligarchy profit from drought because they sell water at extremely inflated price to charge the ordinary working person for a glass of water. It's the Blue Gold to them. They can't think any higher than that.*

C: *Yes, I heard about this, I read that the Bush family purchased 150,000 acres of water rich land in Paraguay after already having purchased another 150,000 acres. I expect in anticipation of man-made drought.*

Trevor: *It is their dream to get people to pay extortionate prices for a glass of water, which is their priority*

C: *Yes, privatisation of water has been going on since dear old Margaret Thatcher brought the concept into reality. I was following this at the beginning of the millennium as George Monbiot gave a great talk at the World Social Forum on this issue. He explained how poor African families were being forced to have water meters installed into their homes, when they could barely afford to pay the fees to keep these water meters running which means they were forced to go and drink dirty water, which then made them sick with Cholera, so privatisation being forced in this way on third world countries is the most inhuman thing the western world could do.*

Trevor: *Especially when this technology is available, with a primitive airplane and one of my tubes they can have all the water they can use. The oligarchy is at pains to prevent my doing that and it is really surprising that I am still alive, all things considered.*

C: *Yes, fantastic you have angels taking good care of you. This situation has to change, for example say if someone educated themselves on this particular science of the aether, and a local* *community tried out small experiments from the ground, if local people could generate rain from a P-Gun is that possible?*

Trevor: *They could do that or they could use primitive methods of accumulating rain, that has happened in the UK, Cornwall, there are special types of rocks that help accumulate rain, but obviously that is not a mass solution, how do you get water into London for example? A colossal city like that, you have to have access to the overhead, where it is all stored for you, all you have to do is get it down! And we know how to do that now.*

C: *You have shown that your system works well in tropical rain, Demayer's work in Africa, he has done some work to make rain there.*

Trevor: *Yes, he made huge lakes in north eastern Africa, it can be done, and governments just don't want to do it. They are afraid of the oligarchy as that is how they lose power, displease the oligarchy and out they go even if by murder, it calls for constant agitation and by dedicated people to get this into human use, the fact that this is so simple is a great thing, it is a marvellous thing really.*

C: *Yes, this is what makes me passionate about getting people to know your work, obviously there are people out there who do know your work. There is a slow gathering towards sustainability that people are starting to realise is a way to release ourselves as currency from the archaic capitalistic system, if we can use these techniques in areas where we have new sustainable or self-sustaining communities that are able to develop their own alternative energy, their own water technology with your rain engineering techniques, if people were able to organise themselves to get together and do that, we would have a blueprint for a new way of living, self-sustainable communities that survive outside these capitalistic systems. That way self-governing communities are free of control by the oligarch.*

Trevor: *There is no doubt about it, the number of people who get in touch with me, who come across my website is certainly quite astonishing. There are too many of them, I can't deal with it really. So, I tell them to read the book and go out and do it. There is* *enough information in the book "The Loom of the Future" and in the videos which I have made, for people to learn and see how to do it. That is perfectly obvious that you could do it, with some intelligence and understanding of the aethers and so forth, they could do it, the thing is most people want someone else to do these things for them, someone else to take the hits.*

C: *You see that is the kind of conditioning embedded in our consciousness to expect everyone else to do these things for us and we really do need to realise that in order to survive and be autonomous we have to educate ourselves.*

Trevor: *Yes that is very true. Yes the book I refer to is "The Loom of the Future," at least prior to airborne development and the airborne use of p-guns automatically made everything else obsolete. The airborne method is so effective, that you wouldn't want to be bothered doing it from the ground, it is far more efficient to put them on an airplane. It would turn out in the long run to be much cheaper, in half an hour of going out on an airborne trip you can make it rain, just about anywhere apart from the Sahara where there is not enough chemical aether to make it rain.*

The Japanese and Chinese may already know that what they call Chi energy in Chinese medicine is also the aether or orgone energy of Wilhelm Reich, all he did was make the chi scientific with his scientific measurements, he proved that chi was real and others pay no attention to his findings, people prefer to leave themselves in the hands of the doctors and be bamboozled by them. That is what the orgone energy is, the chi of Asia in scientific form.

C: *Yes, I have to agree, I studied Qigong and some aspects of Chinese medicine over a year ago, the basics are that the 12 main meridians that run through the human body are chi or orgone pathways for this energy. I started doing the chi and Qigong and it has definitely changed my life, I feel it has restored the life force energy in my lower Dan Tien, I also notice that if I accidentally burn my hand when I have been cooking, it heals a lot quicker. I can also recharge myself energy wise by just doing some Tai chi with particular movements that are based on five thousand year old* *knowledge, the earliest Chinese doctors considered this a science back then.*

Trevor: *Most people don't realise that in China, three thousand years ago, and several thousand years before America was even thought of, that they had a complete pharmacological system that worked that was also based on controlling the chi energy. Whereas, the modern medical profession do not acknowledge chi energy, life force, or anything except pharmaceutical drugs. People are getting upset about the American medical system which is no medical system at all, it just drives people into the clutches of the pharmaceutical industry, which they really need to avoid rather than get into.*

C: *Yes, the American pharmaceutical companies, are only about 80 years old and are already controlling the world! That is a whole other intrepid subject really,*

Trevor: *Yes it is!*

C: *You sent me an interesting article on a book review you did on Dr Batmanghelidj M.D. Featured in The Borderlands Journal.*

Trevor: *He died a few years ago when he just got back from a triumphant tour of Europe, he wanted me to go with him and show my weather films on his program, at that time I had recovered from a stroke and I didn't want to bring it on again, so I said you are best going by yourself and I will see you when you get back, when he got back he was caught in a blizzard in New York state, he contracted pneumonia and passed away and I lost a good friend there. He was marvellous in bringing the importance of water as a healing agent and a conditioning agent for the human organism. We simply do not drink enough water. Most of the diseases we have that we try to defeat with chemicals are overcome by undertaking adequate water intake that is what you have to do. That is what he taught.*

He started researching this when he was in prison in Tehran, they said, 'well you're not such a bad guy we are going to let you out', he said 'no I am going to finish my research, I will stay in for another six months', so he voluntarily stayed there for 6 months until his research on water was completed.

C: *Are you familiar with Dr Masuru Emoto's work on water?*

Trevor: *Yes, particularly on the crystalline forms that can be made to appear out of water, they show the condition of the water and feasibility for consumption and how you can damage water just like you can damage a living organism, you can damage water by mishandling it, even putting it through pipes can damage water structure.*

C: *He was also doing research on how human thoughts and emotions affect water, he took pictures of different crystals produced under different thought vibration, there are pictures of beautiful crystals that emerged from loving thoughts and emotions, then some really distorted and strange looking ones from some very negative thought forms. That is really fascinating when you think about how much water we have in the human body, and therefore we are affecting the water structures in cells in our bodies by our feelings and emotions and how that in turn has an effect on our health as well.*

Trevor: *Yes, correct.*

C: *Have you heard of the work of Doctor Abrams?*

Trevor: *He was a San Francisco-based Doctor, and at a university in Europe, Abrams was hated by the medical profession here, they did everything to undo him. He laid the basis for Dr Ruth B. Drown, who was a good friend and one whom I knew very well. It is in the book The Cosmic Pulse of Life, the complete story of my relationship with her.*

Dr Abrams found that live tissue and diseased tissue had two different rates of vibration, he went on to test this to verify what the vital force was in any particular organ or tissue and he developed a system on which Ruth Drown built her work, she became world famous in her time, for developing what we can now see is 21st Century medicine. But she was also bombarded and blasted by the modern medical bunch here in a most unbelievable way - which seems to be the normal response when someone has something useful for mankind, this is driven by the anti-mankind forces which exist in the world and you have to push against them.

Ruth Drown took cross-sectional pictures, of the human body, I saw her do this many times, these pictures even today were far superior to what you get from an MRI scan, they were cross-sections that could go right through bone and blood and anything like that, and you could see everything. She was a marvellous woman.

C: *What kind of technology was she using?*

Trevor: *The technology has been placed under the term of Radionics since, she was unique in that she was able to take photographs with her equipment. These were on 8 by 10 cut film. You would take them out of the processing and put them on an X-ray viewer and look at them just like you would an X-ray and they were cross-sectional. One of these photos is in my book The Cosmic Pulse of Life. The picture can be easily understood by an ordinary person in as much it was a photograph of a tooth that was abscessed, you could see the lines of the tooth and the way it sits in the gum and the veins, in the pulp of the tooth and these pictures today are far superior to what you get with an MRI or anything else. She took thousands of pictures like this but never got any recognition for her work at all - which is terrible.*

So anybody who thinks that this is a free country or that sort of thing, must understand that it is just not true. She eventually had a stroke after she was arrested and thrown into jail at the age of 72 and before she could go to trial on trumped up charges that they were going to attack her with, she simply died. I figured she had just had enough of mankind. She died as a consequence of being assailed that way.

C: *What did they charge her with?*

Trevor: *They hired a person to pose as a patient that went to her and complained of certain pain and illness, and got her to make a diagnosis and then they said "well, this is not true, this person doesn't have these things, we have all these doctors that says she* *doesn't and yet you say she does, so we are going to charge you with fraud." she was torpedoed.*

C: *Usually the way they do it, to sabotage people's work they set them up.*

Trevor: *People have told me that the story of Ruth P. Drown in The Cosmic Pulse of Life is invaluable in itself. I had no doubt that she was a really superior individual. To be associated with her was one of the high points of my own life.*

C: *The work you have done is also very pioneering, which is based on the work of other pioneers so it doesn't surprise me that you have been associated with such people.*

Trevor: *Pioneering is no piece of cake I'll tell you!*

C: *Exactly, it is not an easy path which you have chosen.*

Trevor: *Well, it has cost me a lot in many ways and I have paid a very heavy price for it, I will say that at least I did my part.*

C: *I am sure that one day your work will be acknowledged for what it is worth and it will be appreciated, now is the time as the veils are crumbling.*

Trevor: *There is a group down in Brisbane, Australia, that has really comprehended the magnitude of my contributions and what could be done with them and they are going to put it together into a film that can be distributed throughout the world. At this time they have a big problem down there with smog, well, I took care of Los Angeles smog in 1990 in the most successful operation we ever had, Operation Clincher using aetheric rain-engineering, and it wasn't looked at. We couldn't interest the anti-smog bureaucracy at all, while they were making statements about what a wonderful improvement it was, they had been told that we were going to do this. Yet they did not react to it at all, instead they exulted as though they had done it, then the next year the smog went up by 12 percent.*

C: *Again they profit from pollution as well as drought, don't they?*

Trevor: *That is correct. The big capitalists want it to go on just like it is. If they had taken up my technology we wouldn't have any smog at all. And they won't have it in Brisbane either as those guys are going to go ahead and install it whether the government likes it or not. Nobody has to have smog, it is easy to get rid of it.*

C: *Jose Escamilla was the person that introduced me to your work, he was the first person I interviewed about his documentary 'Moon Rising', he referred me to your work when you started filming these plasma orbs or 'critters' as you call them back in the 1950s, is that right?*

Trevor: *Yes that is right, 1957.*

C: *So could you tell us how you started filming these creatures in the unseen realm?*

Trevor: *The situation in the early fifties was, whatever factual information there was regarding the UFOs, was in the hands of the government and they were not handing it out. They were hushing up everything to do with the UFOs and the possibility of there ever being interplanetary spaceships or anything like that. There was a complete information lock-down altogether.*

I directed my attention to one particular fact seen all over the world, this was where the instances when unidentified flying objects that were in the sky would disappear while they were under observation. They didn't go over the horizon or anything like that, they just vanished. Similarly, there were objects that came into being right out of nowhere. This was another thing that was reported repeatedly and nobody had any explanation for it. So we had objects materialising and dematerialising, in the skies of the Earth. At that time, I was investigating where had they gone to and where had they come from?

So I got some infrared film to see if they were not just around the corner somewhere and that is how it started with Dr Jim Woods, a local chiropractor, helping me. We started going out to the Californian High Desert and taking pictures of empty sky, we never saw anything with the naked eye but we have all these pictures of

UFOs in the infrared. So, that proved that is where they went. Into the infrared, therefore they had an existence in the infrared and could be accessed there. I have no doubt that the government had subsequently got on to this, otherwise they wouldn't have made that million dollar camera to go into the ultra-violet region. Remember that ultra-violet is a harmonic of infra-red.

C: *With the Infra-red and ultra-violet is it only heat bodies that show up on the camera, not dust as some people claim?*

Trevor: *Yes that is right. We know that from experience that they are there pretty much all of the time and that you can get pictures of them virtually any time that you want. It helps if you make a focus of yourself for them, that allows them to see you from the infrared which we did with the aid of the device called the star exercise, where you circulated your body in a methodical way and each time you got into one of these resonance points, you could feel a pulse going out from you and you would go to maybe a hundred repetitions of this exercise by which time you could hardly even move, you had the system wound up so tightly it was difficult to move, the UFOs would come and look at you. There was something that went across from the infra-red and the red, which enabled them to see you and to oscillate around you, we got pictures like that. It was very far out work for that time, a lot could be done with it today if you had the funding which is not available for anything like that, and it is only available for people that want to hurt other people.*

C: *Could you explain what you mean by 'star exercise'?*

Trevor: *The star exercise is fully laid out in the Cosmic Pulse of Life, spread your legs comfortably apart, hold your arms out parallel to the ground then you oscillate your body through the various cardinal points and build up a force especially if you go over a hundred repetitions*

C: *Sounds like another way to move chi through the body, when you do a lot of Qigong, you certainly feel that pulse, Qigong and Tai chi has its roots in ancient shamanic dancing, where a lot of spinning was involved, the earlier civilisations must have been more aware of the Earth and cosmic energies, there are chi energies from the Earth* *that spiral up into the ether and spiral down, you can see that with the way trees and some plants grow with the Fibonacci spiral forms. I am wondering if your star exercise was agitating some chi flow there.*

Trevor: *I am sure it does, I am sure that what you feel is an accumulation of chi, it also focuses all of your energy to a central point as normally you are scattered all over the place. The star exercise is to focus all your vehicles into a central point and it is very beneficial. It allows the UFOs to see your energy field build up around you across the barrier between the infrared and invisible realms.*

C: *Going back to the famous tether incident where we can see these plasma organisms or UFOs swimming around this twelve mile long tether. Jose Escamilla used the video in his documentary Moon Rising, to show examples of these creatures as he had discovered images of them in the thin atmosphere of the moon too with his colour photographs of the moon.*

Trevor: *Actually they were 80 miles away in that ultra-violet film, but you can figure out from the twelve mile long tether that these creatures are at least two miles in diameter!*

C: *I tried to present that video to people but they say, that is just dust,*

Trevor: *In infrared and ultra-violet, there is no way out of it being anything but what it is. I don't know how that video got into the public domain, I really don't. It is beyond argument though.*

C: *Have you heard of the increased sightings of plasma orbs over the UK? These you can see, they are usually orange in colour, and they look like they are on fire. One expert on these orbs is Susan Joy Renison and she claims that they are conscious beings, alive, accumulating because of the Earth changes here, she was saying that the Russians were doing observations and probably using your type of camera, they are seeing a mass exodus of some organisms and others coming into the Earth's atmosphere, which they filmed using the infrared technologies. So there is a shift of organisms* *invisible to the human eye that are leaving and entering the planet's atmosphere. What is your opinion on that?*

Trevor: *I have had contact with the orb phenomenon, through a medical doctor in Northern California whom is a friend of mine, I have a package of pictures here. So they are not news to me, he has them around his house up there and his daughter can call them in so to speak. So they come in answer to her call, they are clearly elemental beings of some sort. I have seen enough of them to know they are absolutely authentic. No argument about that. They are all colours, green, and blue, red all over. They are seen all over the world, in every country, I don't think there is a country that hasn't been visited by the orbs. The scientific community are very slow to catch onto this and would likely to dismiss anyone that did tackle the subject and that person would possibly have problems getting a job.*

C: *You have obviously heard about crop circles that we have here, especially in the western part of the UK, I have a friend that went down to Wiltshire specifically to investigate them, he stayed at a pub bed and breakfast, the next morning a crop circle had formed in the field next to the house he was staying in and he had seen a smaller orb, usually white light, the people in the countryside have seen them so often, especially around the time these crop circles are formed that it is taken for granted. What is your opinion on them?*

Trevor: *Yes I have seen the smaller ones, they are about six inches in diameter. They are part of the array of life on Earth, I made this point in The Cosmic Pulse of Life about the cave drawings down in Cantabria, Spain, which go back to three thousand years BC, the UFOs are represented in among drawings of ibex and bison. Palaeolithic man knew that UFOs were here, it is the scientific people that are behind the times.*

C: *I have seen some petroglyphs with spirals in the sky as well, which is interesting since the Norway Spiral's appearance, what is your perspective on that incident?*

Trevor: I don't know anything about that, but I know that the human eye is just a tiny little crack, into the whole of the vibrational spectrum.

C: *Yes, we are very arrogant to measure everything by the human five senses to completely negating a whole spectrum of organisms and creatures and energy and ether, which exist outside the measurements that we have founded science upon.*

Trevor: *Yes, we are a very arrogant species, we would do well once in a while to realise the period on which materialistic science rests. It is not more than three hundred years at the most, It has been an existence, that is nothing compared to the age of the cosmos, even what we admit to, when you figure we are looking through a very small chink in the visible range, to what is visible and what isn't and we see almost nothing. Then we look down a microscope to intensify the vision, and there is a whole world down there, that we didn't know existed, but there it is. Well you can do the same thing when you expand the sensitivity of the human eye with things like the video tape that the American government made, stuff exists there all the time, it hasn't come from anywhere else. It is not something that came from Mars or Venus, or Pluto it is just part of this world, part of the whole world, we are very reluctant to advance to this realisation. We are more concerned with how we can transform what we learn into destructive knowledge.*

C: *One of the stories that you wrote about that grabbed my attention was the Morley Martin, looking down the microscope and finding these creatures just coming out of the stone. He died in 1938 and published a small brochure in 1934 called 'The reincarnation of animal and plant life from protoplasm isolated from the mineral kingdom'.*

Trevor: *Coming out of Precambrian Azoic Rocks, we need to rewrite all the biology books, these predate life on Earth, Azoic rocks have never disclosed any fossils and Morely Martin discovers these creatures. There was a naval commander present there, he looked under the microscope and saw claws materialising, legs sprouting and watched a creature crawl out of view of the microscope field. Other scientists criticised his findings by saying he didn't use a proper sterile environment. He did everything to incandescence and still these things appeared.*

C: *As you say, it is not where there is life, it is where is there not life? And this is the foundation for all your amazing work Trevor. You have given a great gift to people and it is a great honour to interview you and share your knowledge. We need to get people to look at your work and start a whole orgone revolution.*

Trevor: *Thank you, we can talk again when we get the results of the Smog cleaning project in Brisbane.*

ENDNOTES: Chapter 6

1. The live recorded interview between the author and Trevor James Constable can be accessed here. https://sailingbeyondknowledge.wordpress.com/2010/03/04/exploring-the-cosmic-pulse-of-life-with-trevor-james-constable/

2. Trevor James Constable's Etheric Rain Engineering site .rainengineering.com/

Trevor's recommended reading:

Guenther Wachsmuth (1932) *The Etheric Formative Forces in Cosmos, Earth and Man.* BSF.

Ernst Marti, MD (1984) *The Four Ethers*. Schaumberg Publications,

Wilhelm Reich (1940) *The Function of the Orgasm-The Discovery of the Life Energy*. Farrar, Straus and Giroux

Ernst Lehrs (1930) *Man or Matter*. Create Space Publication

Rudolph Stciner (1920) *The Warmth Course*. Mercury Press.

Morley Martin (1934) *The Reincarnation of Animal and Plant Life from Protoplasm Isolated from the Mineral Kingdom.*

Meade Layne (1950). *The Morley Martin Experiments and the Experiments of Dr Charles w. Littlefield.* BSRA.

Ivan T.Sanderson (1967) Uninvited Visitors.

Wilhelm Reich

http://www.wilhelmreichmuseum.org/biography.html

The Ether, Consciousness, Radionics, Ancient Knowledge, Light & Electricity by Thomas Brown. thomasbrown.org

Trevor James Constable's books

Trevor J. Constable (1975) *Cosmic Pulse of Life.* Published by Merlin Press, Tustin, California. Known as the "underground classic." Republished 1977 in hardback by Neville Spearman, Ltd., London. Revised and enlarged version published in 1990 by Borderland Sciences Research Foundation. Since reprinted.

d. Trevor. J. Constable. (1994) *Loom of the Future*. Borderland Sciences Research Foundation. Comprehensive overview of TJC'S weather engineering work since its inception. In the unique format of a giant, heavily illustrated interview. Over 130 pictures (misc. articles written for the Borderland Journal and other magazines)

VIDEOS:

1. ETHERIC WEATHER ENGINEERING ON THE HIGH SEAS 1991 Produced and directed by TJC, offered through Borderands on the world public market.

2. A.E.R.E.O. Airborne Etheric Rain Engineering Operations. 2000. Directed by TJC, produced by Etheric Rain Engineering Pte Ltd. Singapore. Corporate video demonstrating airborne etheric rain engineering without chemicals or electric power.

Chapter 7: Introducing Alternative Energy

The USA which is only 5 percent of the world's population, consumes 25 percent of the world's nuclear power, so the amount of nuclear waste created per person per year is around 40 grams, which is an incredible amount, it seems lunacy when you learn that it takes 3 million years for nuclear waste to decay. There are 438 nuclear power stations on planet Earth, One nuclear power station generates 3,000 tons of nuclear waste per year, this means that altogether one million, three hundred and fourteen thousand tons of nuclear waste is generated globally each year, it can cost up to 20 billion dollars to build a nuclear waste repository. There is no accounting for the millions of nuclear war heads in existence which cost trillions to maintain. So why are billions being spent to turn planet Earth into a nuclear time bomb? All of this, while those of us in the Free Energy movement are called crackpots and lunatics?

Mainstream scientific establishments and universities are funded by giant corporations and government departments which will only support the agenda of the government and superpowers, therefore anyone who invents a clean and free energy device or a cure for cancer is immediately a threat to the centralisation of power. The first step to understanding why these inventors are suppressed is to understand the politics and economic motives behind centralised government systems.

There is no need to power our cars and trucks with fossil fuels .We already have clean free energy options and we have had them for 180 years, choices which have been violently and systematically suppressed by the oligarchy while they profit from pollution and drought

For decades the oil and electrical power companies and their allies in the U.S. Government have viciously and thoroughly suppressed new energy inventions which threaten the oil and power monopolies. For example, the U.S. Patent Office has unfairly classified 5000 energy patents as 'secret'. They have also denied 650,000 Free Energy Patents.

What does 'Free-Energy' really mean?

Most Engineers and Physicists are aware of the Law of Conservation of Energy which says "you cannot take more out of a system than you put into a system′, almost true but not quite, as you can take more out of a system than **you** put into the system. There are many ways of doing this, as energy is already all around us, and this is what the field of Free-Energy Science deals with. Most people are aware of solar, wind, geothermal and hydropower power systems. A simple example is wind power, the energy flowing in, comes from the environment and what comes out is increase in power and energy from a simple wind generator. The same happens with solar energy generation. There is a positive outlook for the booming [1]Solar Photovoltaics industry which will by 2015, exceed the nuclear power energy production.

Some people think of Free-Energy as being a futuristic concept, such as the more exotic kinds of Free-Energy like The "Hutchison Effect" and his Zero-Point Energy Converter Cells - Credited with the discovery of a highly-anomalous electromagnetic effect which causes the levitation of heavy objects; jellification of metals; and fusion of dissimilar materials such as metal and wood; anomalous heating of metals without burning adjacent material; spontaneous fracturing of metals; both temporary and permanent changes in the crystalline structure and physical properties of metals; and other effects resulting from what is believed to be a very complex scalar-wave interaction between electromagnetic fields and matter.

Tesla was at the forefront of such discoveries but he also was aware of the potential malevolent use of some of these energy systems and therefore kept much of this research quiet, then of course much of his work and research was destroyed when the government realised how his work could implicate their agenda to seize a fortune from Grid-Wired Electricity at the closing of a switch. Scientists rely on government funding for their research. If the resulting research and inventions are not on a par with the government's power agendas, then the scientist will have his/her research grants and funds and academic privileges cut off then facing public ridicule, slander and long-term unemployment. Science has been controlled and shaped in this way for a hundred years. What students are taught in the physics laboratory at school and university is not the full reality.

What most do not know, is that alternative energy was discovered more than 180 years ago and along with the points which I highlighted earlier, is a major threat to destabilising current government powers which have been profiting out of needlessly destroying the environment for oil and nuclear power, while we have had this technology all along. Most foundations, NGOs and charities do not wish to tackle anything to do with Free-Energy, nor do the chief editors of publishing companies, newspapers, most magazines and journals, due to the sensitivity of its suppression by governments and the fear of facing the same ridicule and damage to public image. Many organisations are afraid to tackle the reality of the issue for fear of being discredited, publicly humiliated or cut off from grants and government support. So Free Energy remains this mysterious exotic dream to most people, yet functioning devices exist today in an array of options.

Energy surrounding our bodies makes our heads be at a higher voltage than the voltage at our feet. If you connect high and low voltage points with a wire, you get a current flowing through the wire. Hermann Plauson, a German scientist, showed how simply you can pull energy out of the air or aether with an aerial which can have an output of about a kilowatt. With a group of such tall aerials, hundreds of kilowatts can be extracted in spite of the fact that you, personally, have provided no input power at all. This is a really simple example of a basic device. You can get the details of a "Plauson Ariel'' from [2]Patrick Kelly's website or the [3]Overunity forum. Have you ever wondered why do we have wireless internet but not wireless electricity? It makes no sense whatsoever....electricity is everywhere. Wilhelm Reich and Tesla both discovered this.

There are many ways in which you can tap into this energy, and many Free Energy scientists have achieved over-unity (taking more power out of a system than put into a system) by doing this. A good introduction for those new to this concept is the transcript I have included from the recorded interview with author and Free-Energy expert Patrick Kelly, which you will find later on in this chapter.

Consider the disharmony of evolving technologies in terms of comparing how far we have come with computer technology, wireless internet, and solar power and yet we are still driving around fossil fuel-guzzling, heavy, clunking bits of metal spewing out carbon dioxide, carbon monoxide and other pollutants.

British Shell Petroleum, which is just one of dozens of different oil companies, makes a net profit of about [4]one hundred million pounds an hour. That is, every hour of every day of every week of every month of every year, they get an extra one hundred million pounds to play with. Governments, political stakeholders, oil investors and oil companies alike don't feel comfortable with us knowing this, and they would be quite upset if an inventor comes along and says "hey wouldn't you like to buy this water-fuel powered car or domestic power generator run by magnets, which will only cost you a few thousand pounds and produces all the electricity that you will ever want, no fuel needed, wouldn't that be great?" The answer is that the oil companies would **not** like it at all, and the people who would like it even less are the government, who take in around 85 percent of the cost that we pay at the fuel pump as tax. The executive oil directors and governments will do what they can to prevent any one of us owning a car that runs on anything but oil-based fuel. This power and profit-driven suppression of new alternative technologies for energy efficient vehicles, is the reason why we do not see them offered for sale. It is also why many are not granted patents or given the opportunity to be made available for public sale on the 'free market'.

[5]Some key government figures are arm in arm with oil companies worldwide. Politicians and oil barons are often one and the same. Just take a look at the Bush family, while [6]Tony Blair was deeply involved with Egypt and Israel's gas industry as an energy advisor, it was recently revealed that they are involved with plundering Gaza's gas ocean-based reserves, which Israel is planning on selling to Egypt. The Labour Party, (Tony Blair's political party), has received up to 2.5 million pounds in donations in less than a year,

from energy giants as a means to influence a privileged few in their environmental policies to become more flexible for energy industries. It is not the focus of this book to go into details about these examples of underhanded corruption, but it is important to note because this is one of the main driving forces of environmental exploitation. You could say that the most powerful government positions are mostly filled by those who either run oil companies or are connected to the families of those who run oil companies. Their goal is to make sure that our society stays in a kind of stasis, dependent on oil and gas, as it keeps the present governments in power, and generates for them, a huge financial profit at a cost we all are paying for, by global environmental destruction. This addiction to power and money through oil sales, is an addiction each of us are a part of, even if it is involuntary, but it is costing us the very Earth on which we live.

Four years ago [7]Scott Brusaw from California, USA, gave a talk with Ted Talks, (an organisation, that sponsors people to talk about their ideas and projects), presenting the 'Solar Roadway Project', which is a project where 'green' Engineers have been working to produce solar-powered roads and cars that could even help power homes and businesses. [8]The 2013, 3,000 km world Solar Challenge recently took place in Australia and was won by a Dutch Solar company named Eindhoven, which has built a solar-powered vehicle called 'Stella' and which is designed for families, they will perform the same challenge this year (2015), why again? It is important to keep demonstrating that solar and water cars can run as efficiently as the conventional car, as with many alternative fuel cars, it is possible that in a few years' time, we will probably see these car fade into the background, a fate that has already been the case of countless other green vehicles produced over the past decades. For example, [9]Stanley Meyer of America, invented his Water Fuel Cell and water-powered car and he was granted patents in 1989, since then some other water-fuel cars have been built by other inventors. Just last year, members of the Pakistani parliament, scientists, and students alike watched in awe as [10]Waqar Ahmad, a Pakistani engineer, successfully demonstrated a water-powered car in Islamabad. With just one litre of water, Ahmad claims that a 1000 cc car could cover a distance of 40 km, or a motorbike could travel 150 km.

In 2011, Japan invented a powerful water car produced by a company called [11]Genepax, a Japanese company that unveiled a car that can run on river, rain or sea water, and even run on Japanese tea. The first compressed air car model to get media attention was in 1996, though there have been much earlier models in existence, in 2003, the French produced the Compressed Air Car, [12]Moteur Development International, and Peugeot Citroen both have compressed air cars which they plan to market to the public in 2016.

With this in mind, we can consider that we no longer need oil from the rainforest or the oceans. What we do need is to keep the rainforest and oceans preserved, perhaps via an international law that overrules political and corporate decision makers to protect the environment from Ecocide. The conservation of our environment could be seen as a matter of international security since destroying our environment in turn destroys the future of human survival. Is not the future of the world's rainforests and oceans, a matter of human survival? With our growing awareness, we each individually have a pressing responsibility to push for a transition from an oil-based economy to an ecologically-sustainable economy.

Free Energy is the only solution to ending the destruction of our environment, there are already many advanced solutions in the form of alternative technologies. Solutions that should have been available to humanity a long time ago, and yet these are conveniently overlooked by global decision makers, which leads to the simple question "***why?***"

Corporations are currently assigned more rights than human beings have. Human rights continue to deteriorate and while some might think it is debateable, legislations are currently being pushed to implement that Planet Earth be given the same right as people, since the Earth is a living macro-organism that supports all life, yet corporations are now considered the legal fiction of a 'person' in the court of law and receive more privileges than people or the planet. Unfortunately corporations and governments are addicted to their positions of control and power, going so far as attempting to own human life; making us and our fellow plant and animal species a lucrative commodity to destructive levels of making us all part of a grand laboratory experiment to be profited from.

It is important to highlight the fact that mainstream science taught in schools and universities is only a tiny segment of a larger science that continues to be kept hidden from humanity. This tiny part that we are familiar with, is used as a propaganda tool to keep the governments in power and people from believing that Free-Energy already exists all around us.

It is necessary to tell people about these suppressed sciences. People in the academic sector live in fear of this knowledge or speaking openly about these issues, especially to fellow environmental scientists or physicists. Free-Energy science is rarely acknowledged by most environmental campaigners or scientists or organisations who talk about improving the environment with alternative energy. Greenpeace do great work and started out as a small group of radical investigative journalists motivated to make radical changes, now they won't even take the subject of Free-Energy seriously, perhaps because they are put off by the implications of this subject and fear it would reduce public support and donations if they did take up the campaign. Despite this, public awareness is growing and those of us that have the knowledge, feel an intense desire to pass it on and share it with many more that are up for the challenge. We must embrace a change from the current energy control monopoly which is destroying the planet .

Only specific institutions and scientists are chosen to be given funding if their work complies with, and supports, the government agenda to keep itself in power and control the world's resources. Real science is suppressed and never funded as it will empower humanity and disable governments from their current power-system control over ordinary people.

[13]Paramahamsa Tewari is Chief Project Engineer of the Kaiga Project, Karwar, India, he and many other alternative energy scientists have already disproved the mainstream beliefs of the laws of physics. He states "*It has been hitherto believed in physics that the total electric charge in the Universe is a constant quantity, and if*

additional charge appears in some region, it is only at the expense of the charge deficit in some other regions. It is a basic law that electric charge is conserved and cannot be destroyed or created. Precise experiments on a Space Power Generator (SPG) which has been now further developed to demonstrate the commercial viability of the newly discovered phenomenon of space power generation however, totally violate the existing law of conservation of charge, by generating output electrical power much in excess of the input electrical power. Since electric charge is a form of basic energy, the law of conservation of energy will need to be enlarged to incorporate in it the dynamics of absolute vacuum which in a state of rotation generates a fundamental field to produce electrical charge and energy."

One of the most obvious problems adding to our planetary crisis is the issue of Energy, Petroleum, and Gas, Nuclear Power, and Hydro-electric power. There is no longer any need for the current archaic environmentally destructive method of harnessing energy while these other repressed forms work more efficiently and could solve all of our problems.

In my small university we were taught that Sir James Lovelock was the founder of the Gaia Theory, where Earth being made up of small ecological units that are like the organs of the greater living Earth, then in the early 2000s Lovelock suddenly began sponsoring nuclear power as the best energy source! This made no sense whatsoever. Years on after the world has seen many environmental disasters involving nuclear energy after the recent worldwide spread of radiation from Fukushima; Japan's continuing nuclear meltdown that contaminates the ocean, yet it is very difficult to find accurate measurements of radiation contamination that is detrimental to sea life and to human life, despite sea mammals, birds and fish continually washing up en mass dead or starving onto beaches. Fukushima has proved how potentially dangerous nuclear power is, we all know this and live with it on a day to day basis as if desensitised to the extreme danger we put ourselves and the Earth in by using nuclear energy.

In 2010, I sought out an independent unbiased Free Energy expert that had a diverse knowledge of all the Free Energy inventors and devices in existence, we conducted a recorded interview of which the transcript is taken from below.

Scratching the Surface of Free Energy with Patrick Kelly. June 4th 2010.

After merely scratching the surface with an introduction to [14]Free-Energy, Patrick Kelly shares his knowledge and expertise on Free-Energy devices and the tribulations and challenges that inventors go through whilst attempting to make their designs available to the world. Patrick Kelly has compiled an amazing resource of information and eBooks along with offering many Free-Energy related patents which researchers can download free from his websites. Patrick Kelly's background is in engineering.

"one of the well-known laws in engineering is the "Law" of Conservation of Energy, which says you cannot take more out of a system than you put into it, which is almost true but not quite. You can't take more energy out of a system than is in it, but you don't necessarily have to put it into the system in the first place. I was not aware of this until in 1985 I was alerted to the existence of Free-Energy by a TV documentary called "It Runs on Water". The program itself was not well presented or helpful in encouraging further research by the viewer, however it showed the work of Stan Meyer of the United States, where he demonstrated that it is possible to split water rather than breaking it down using electrolysis. Water-splitting is a system which requires far less energy than electrolysis. I saw his experiments on a video copy of the TV programme which I had made, but I couldn't quite make out the patent number which I needed in order to do further research on his device, so I called the patent office and explained the problem at which point they laughed and said 'we've had dozens of calls for this, what we will do is send you a list of 40 of his patents and you can then choose which ones you want to order'.

It was from then on I was aware that there was such a thing as Free Energy. If you think about it, the evidence is all around you. You can draw energy from the wind and for that, you do not have to put any energy into it as the energy comes flowing in from the environment. The same with water, you can use the water in a river to turn a water wheel and that will generate energy that you can use day in, day out with no need for any kind of fuel. The same applies to tides, using tidal energy to power generators when the tide goes in and out. You can generate a large amount of energy from waves using your own equipment or a generator that can be built into floor of the seabed. You can get lots of other energy coming in free from the environment, sunlight which will heat water, power engines or generate electricity from solar panels. There is Geothermal energy where the difference between the temperature deep down in the Earth and at the surface, is sufficient to drive generators. Very simple and obviously, the sun shines on plants and they grow, when you can dry them and burn them you can get energy from that 'biomass'. There are other sources of free-energy. When I was young there were no real electronic components available. We built crystal radio receivers, from wire and a crystal. I did not realise it at the time that was a key component for one method of extracting energy from the environment. There is a patent by Raymond Phillips which shows how to take an aerial, choose any radio station, whatever frequency you like, tune it and produce a current which will run lights and charge batteries, that is a low power operation but it does work.

You can also pull energy from the general environment itself and conventional science will always assure you that there is a very large difference in voltage as you rise up from the surface of the Earth, so much so that if you are standing on the ground, your head is probably several hundred volts, higher voltage than your feet. You know what happens when you connect a higher voltage with a lower voltage, you produce a current which you can use to power a light bulb or charge a battery, now the same thing happens in the environment, if you have several hundred volts at your head and zero volts at your feet , then you can use a motionless device to operate on that voltage difference and so can power equipment if you understand the technique. There is a patent which is very informative on this subject from a German man called Herman Plauson and he shows a variety of ways to capture and use this energy. You put up an aerial, and using an Earth connection you can pull a lot of power out of the air with no input power at all! So this very simple method demonstrates that there is energy all around us, energy which can be harnessed and used. When I started compiling my research there was barely anything available about it, now I update my research about 70 times a year, it is an intriguing subject"

C - *What is your experience and knowledge of Free Energy Suppression?*

Patrick - *Suppression is widespread and very violent. This is very understandable because when you think about it, a company like British Shell Petroleum, which is just one of dozens of different Oil Companies, make a net profit of many millions of US dollars per hour, every hour of every day of every week of every month of every year. You can easily understand that they are going to be very upset if someone comes along and says "hey wouldn't you like to buy this generator? This generator will only cost you two thousand dollars and produces all the electricity you will ever want, it uses no fuel, you don't have to buy oil, you can run an electric car on this device, without having to buy any more oil, wouldn't that be great?" The answer is that the oil company would* ***not*** *like it, and the people that would like it even less are the government. The government is taking around 85 percent of the cost that you pay at the fuel pump as tax. The government are not going to be happy if you decide you can run a car without buying oil at all. In the UK they have a pilot scheme by instead of charging for the oil they are going to charge you to use the roads, it doesn't matter that you have already paid for the construction and maintenance of those same roads, they are still going to charge you for using your own roads. The charges have been as high as £1.20 per mile ($1.60) on a motorway, which means if you want to drive two or three hundred miles to visit family, it is going to cost you hundreds of pounds. I think that they are trialling this system to get it going and tested so that if (actually, when) Free Energy is introduced, they have some other way of extracting money from you.*

I have a friend called Dave Lawton who lives in Wales. He and I have run a couple of Free Energy Conferences in Wales. Dave Lawton has replicated Stan Meyer's water-splitting system using low voltage and very little power. I documented his work and now many people have built water-splitters of their own. Dave went to the local Welsh Authority to see if he could get a grant for another project which he was developing. He then got a visit from two people, unsurprisingly, dressed in black. People who were extremely odd, very peculiar, they asked lots of questions and took his documentation. They went away and said that they would be in touch. After a while, when there was nothing from them, Dave phoned the Environmental Agency and asked about them and the Agency said 'Oh they are not from us at all', "Lawton asked, "well can I have their phone number as they have documents of mine which need to be returned?" They said, "well no, we can't give you their phone number, we are not allowed to do that". Eventually he got a message saying that they had posted his documents back days ago. Yet he had not received anything. He kept pursuing them and eventually he did get his documents back but the post mark showed clearly that it had been posted only 24 hours before. That story is just a gentle one.

A friend of mine in India called Ravi, has replicated Dave's water-splitting cell. He is a Mechanical Engineer and he posted YouTube videos, participated in discussions on forums and became well known. He was then raided by five car loads of people who were supposed to have been from the local Tax Office. Instead of just taking his records, they went into his workshop, they took his materials, they took his water-splitting Cell and they warned him "Don't talk about this cell any more". Eventually he got some of his stuff back, he called the local Tax people and asked them, " What was all that about"...and they said, " Well we are sorry but they were not from us at all". The peculiar thing about this was that Ravi had just finished his experiments on splitting water, and so, when they raided him he had completed that work. However, this is quite typical for inventors and developers who talk about what they are doing. Publicity about free-energy designs is most unwelcome for the oil and taxation people in every country.

A friend of mine called Bill Williams in the USA, produced a simple 'Joe Cell' and attached it to his elderly Ford pick-up truck. A Joe Cell is difficult to get working but Bill found that his truck was acting like a racing car with the slightest touch of the accelerator taking the vehicle from 25 mph to 50 mph in no time at all. So before he came into town he pulled into a lay-by at the side of the road to see if he could somehow tone the device down and make it easier to control in heavy traffic. As he stopped off, a big four wheel drive vehicle, pulled in just in front of him and two men whom were armed with pistols got out and they handed him a dossier two inches thick with photographs of all his family, timetables of where they would be at each moment of each day and they said "You must destroy this cell and stop talking about it or else !!".

Bill didn't take very kindly to that treatment, and unfortunately for them, their timing was wrong because, by co-incidence, the night before he had uploaded to the web some engineering blueprints of how you can make this cell. I had just emailed him and asked "These are very nice do you mind if I put them into my eBook?" And he said "no that is fine go ahead". So the moment that he had alerted us to the attempted intimidation by these people, I spread his information widely on the web and so, some ten thousand people had received a copy that day. The really big advantage of doing that is, that there is no longer any gain in intimidating Bill. If they were to attack him or his family, then they would just be giving a stamp of approval to how good his Joe Cell is. So, as a result, it doesn't pay them to intimidate. However they came back to him again, a couple of weeks later to his house, and he saw them off with a shotgun. He pointed this out to the local Sheriff who was not at all happy about armed men coming in and throwing their weight about in his jurisdiction. They haven't been back since.

Bill has now refined his cell so that it is now connected to the carburettor on his vehicle and now, when he drives around, although the engine is able to draw in fuel as normal, it just doesn't, and as he can drive around without using any fuel at all.

John Bedini in the USA, who is a very gifted man, built a device called a Tesla Switch, he built it into a cigar box as a demonstration unit and showed it at the TeslaTech Conference in the States in 1985. He had this device running self-powered for six months. Two armed thugs visited him, in his workshop. They pushed him up against a wall, shoved a gun in his face and said to him "You will buy gasoline for the rest of your life". They then smashed his Tesla Switch. Even twenty years afterwards, John is reluctant to speak about the Tesla Switch in public, although in private, he calls the circuit "Pure Gold !" That form of intimidation is quite typical of what goes on.

Eugene Mallove, was due to demonstrate a Free Energy device to the US Senate. Just a few days before the demonstration, he was beaten to death in his own backyard, this is the kind of treatment which we get from the opposition.

More recently, Bob Boyce, from the States produced a system which was roughly twelve hundred percent more efficient than Michael Faraday's famous figures for electrolysis of water. Bob's design is effectively, a larger version of Dave Lawton's device using plates instead of tubing. Bob's cell can generate 100 litres of HHO gas mix per minute but that rate is so high, that it is usually eased back to 50 litres per minute, (which is a very serious rate of gas flow). Bob was told by Maj. Todd Hathaway, on behalf of the US Military, that "It is all right to use boosters to improve the miles per gallon performance of vehicles, but you must NOT run a vehicle on water alone". In spite of this, Bob continued to experiment. They then tried to give him a 3.5 year jail term "for running a car on an unapproved fuel". Bob beat the charge in court as he was testing an engine running on HHO gas from his electrolyser cell, in this workshop behind his house and not on the road. They then tried to discredit Bob with a fake commercial booster operation, and failed spectacularly as the HHO community was well aware of Bob's abilities. They attacked him in three other ways and he has now retired to 'hill-billy country' and is no longer active.

The opposition reckon that most people are incapable of making free-energy devices for themselves. Most inventors who make a successful device, usually don't document it. Once they have solved their problem, they usually take it apart and move on to something else that interests them. When I talked to Dave Lawton and discovered that he had managed to replicate Stan Meyer's "Water Fuel Cell", his Cell had already reached his spares box, it was then that I asked him if I could write up about it and put it in my eBook.

Generally speaking as well, Inventors and experimenters like that are incapable of stringing two words together and so, can't describe their developments clearly. Also, people who are gifted with the ability to invent free-energy devices, almost never have any kind of business abilities and frequently, no commercial interest of any kind. This makes them vulnerable to unscrupulous members of the opposition. Inventors are usually driven by curiosity about how the world works more than anything else.

Those are just some of the people who have been threatened, there are a lot of other people whom were not so lucky and ended up like Eugene Mallove. There was a guy who developed a battery, which was credit card size and very powerful. He was murdered at Charlotte Airport. It was made it look like death from a heart attack. They have a longitudinal beam weapon which can do that in about 30 seconds, and like radio waves, a longitudinal beam can pass through walls, never mind the glass of a car window.

C - *You have just confirmed one of my theories.*

Patrick - *What's that?*

C - *That a heart attack can be induced.*

Patrick - *Yes that is right. The covert development in the USA is somewhere between fifty and a thousand years ahead of our normal non-covert technology. If you consider how far we have come in the last hundred years, then try and imagine several hundred years more, you can see the sort of difference that it makes. Everything shown in the Star Trek TV series has been developed for real and kept under wraps as they don't want the public to have this kind of knowledge.*

C- *Please carry on and tell us more about other devices that you have researched and come into contact with.*

Patrick - *We are actually sitting in a sea of energy, we are completely surrounded by energy everywhere. We can pick up that energy if we want, it is called 'ambient background energy' of the environment or the 'zero-point energy field'. This energy is all around us, and if you have a device which is producing an energy output, and then you increase the operating voltage, the output goes up in proportion to the square of the voltage. Similarly, if you increase the frequency at which your device operates, then the output goes up with the square of the frequency. So as an example if you have system that is working at fifty or sixty cycles a second on 12 volts, if you double the voltage and double the frequency, you get sixteen times as much power coming out, which means that if you raise the voltage to 9000 or 10000 volts and increase the frequency to 30000 cycles per second or more, you start producing serious amounts of power. These systems were promoted by a man called Donald Smith in the USA, he produced many different designs, some of which have the potential to produce a hundred kilowatts or more, just straight out of what appears to be the air! This is very straightforward science, however most people are not familiar with this type of science due to careful suppression over the last hundred years.*

The Casimir Effect for example is where two plates are close together, there is a force pushing them towards each other, the gap between them should be wider, but they move towards each other, this is due to the zero point energy field moving in all directions equally at the same time, when it hits one of the plates, some of the energy is absorbed by the atoms and molecules in the plate itself, just a very tiny amount. The same happens to the other plate, so they are getting slightly more push, from outside the gap than they are from inside the gap and that makes them move together slightly, which is also the cause of gravity. For example, if you have a pendulum near a very large mountain, the pendulum does not hang vertically downwards, but instead, it gets pushed towards the mountain slightly and so does not hang vertically downwards. The same zero-point energy flowing through the mountain, adds energy to the material making up the mountain, and so maintains the energy level of the atoms and molecules in the mountain.

C -*Some people say that Free-Energy is not actually free, but instead, it is part of a fractal system, therefore taxing the Earth's gravity field, what is your view on this?*

Patrick - *Let me put this in context for you, Oliver Heaviside who was a major expert in this subject (and who, incidentally came up with the famous* $E=mC^2$ *equation copied years later by Einstein) calculated the amount of energy, that is contained in every single 1 cubic centimetre anywhere in the universe, and that amount of energy is sufficient to create all of the visible matter in all of the universe. You could really never deplete the energy by using it, even if you used it for more than a thousand million years. There is another rule of thumb called a "law" by the ignorant, namely, that you can neither create or destroy energy. Now if that is the case, there is no way that anything you do could affect the energy of the Earth, the solar system or the universe. Not a chance. People talk about 'using up' energy, or 'consuming' energy, which is ridiculous. They say that a hundred watt light bulb consumes energy all the time that it is switched on. It doesn't !! There is no such thing as 'consuming energy'. You can actually extract energy from gravity. Hydroelectric schemes do that. Waterwheels do that. Simple mechanical mechanisms such as William Skinner's device do that, but it really doesn't matter as 'gravity' is not actually a force but instead is just a tiny imbalance in the zero-point energy field and so can never, ever, be depleted or reduced.*

C– *Is it part of our conditioning to think this?*

Patrick - *Yes absolutely, people who think that way are just not familiar with the reality of the situation, all you can do with energy is convert it from one form to another, and if you are slick you can convert it from the other form back into its original form, you can do useful work in both directions, it is quite straightforward to do that. One way to access this 'ambient background energy' that we are talking about here is through magnetism. A permanent magnet directs a minute part of the energy field into continuous streams of* *energy which we call 'lines of magnetic force'. The power of a permanent magnet does not come from the magnet itself, but it comes as a continuous stream of energy from the zero-point energy field. There are various ways in which free-energy can be accessed at a practical, usable level. Let me just run through a few of the people who have achieved this in different ways:*

1. Raymond Phillips, his simple aerial produces 5 watts of power which can charge batteries, by taking a radio aerial, turning the signal into a direct current, not using any battery at all, just rectifying what comes down the aerial, this is small time but his patent exists.

2. Bob Boyce's prime interest is in HHO gas. Splitting water into this gas using his system involves using a toroidal transformer on which he winds three separate coils. If you pulse one coil, you actually get a return pulse from all three coils as they are linked magnetically through the toroid. If you then rectify those returning pulses, you get more output power than the power used to generate the initial pulse. There is a guy called Johan in South Africa, who has been using this very technique very effectively. He pulses the three coils simultaneously with three different frequencies of pulses. He has a little girl who drives a toy car powered by an 18 Amp-Hour capacity 12-volt lead-acid battery. She drives her little car around during the day, and then, during the night, her father takes the battery and connects this Bob Boyce battery-charging device to it. The battery powers the circuit and yet the battery gets charged up for the next day, this has already been repeated at least 35 times. According to conventional science, what he does is totally impossible. This proves that present day conventional science is inadequate. It shows us that the theory we are operating from needs to be expanded to cover other systems. Present day theory is based on equations originally defined by James Clerk Maxwell. After his death, some people took his equations and said "it's easier if we don't use this component here because we will never need that", and that was the component that explained mathematically how you can get free-energy. So the actual equations now have had the Free Energy part taken out and the remaining equations are now presented as being Maxwell's but they aren't they are truncated versions of the original equations.

The original equations which Maxwell created showed quite clearly that you could get free energy from the environment if you wanted it.

3. There is a man in Canada called Ron Pugh who has built a very nice John Bedini style battery-pulsing system where he uses one battery to charge a whole bank of large batteries. Once you have finished charging the bank of batteries, you then use one of those batteries to charge another bank of batteries and the remainder of the charged batteries to power your household equipment. Ron gets about 13 times more power coming out that is being put in, this is called the Coefficient Of Performance or "COP". It is the amount of energy which you get out, divided by the amount of energy that ***the user*** *puts in to make it work. Actually, as lead-acid batteries are only 50% efficient, Ron is actually achieving a COP of 26 rather than 13.*

4. For example look at a Solar Panel system. It takes up Free-Energy in the form of sunlight. How much effort do you have to put into generating that energy? None! The sunlight arrives and it generates a current for you. Actually that is one of the techniques you can use with a battery pulsing system, John Bedini has now just gone commercial with a device where you can pulse-charge battery banks even when there is not enough sunlight to allow the conventional battery charging method. The pulsing system doesn't need much voltage. You want the battery that you are charging to be at a different voltage to the one that is driving the system, so you want the charging battery to be "floating". This was the problem with John Bedini's system, you can't power a load with the battery bank while you are charging that same bank of batteries.

5. There is a very simple pulsed flywheel device built of wood that has an excess power of more than 20 watts. It has been built by Mr Tong and is promoted by his colleague Laurence Tseung. It has been on display in Hong Kong for quite some time with people invited to visit and check the performance with their own equipment and meters and even take the device apart to make sure there is nothing hidden. It consists of magnets and coils and a wheel that spins around.

6. There is a device that puts out 100 watts of continuous power and which needs no input power at all. It is called an 'electret'. If you go to your local electrical store and buy a drum of co-axial cable for television aerials, apply a high voltage to it and bake it in an oven for two or three days, let it sit and cool for a week. It then will produce 10,000 volts at ten milliamps, which is 100 Watts. It has no moving parts, and does nothing but pull energy from the environment.

7. A Turkish man called Muammer Yildiz, made a permanent magnet motor and demonstrated it at a Delft University lecture. After ten minutes of the demonstration, he turned it off and took the whole thing apart so it could be examined by the audience to show that there was nothing but permanent magnets powering it. The power output has been calculated as being 300 watts. As it has no need of a power input from the user, it has a COP (Co-efficient of Performance) value of Infinity.

8. I have a video of Floyd Sweet in America, filmed by Tom Bearden, running an early test on a system of his which was called a "vacuum triode amplifier" or "VTA" by Tom. All it is, is a permanent magnet which has three coils wound around it. Floyd powers it with 0.12 milli-watts and yet produced more than 500 watts of AC mains power of 120-volts 60 cycles per second, which is a COP of 3,300, it is not something you can argue about and say well perhaps you are reading the meter wrongly. When the gain is over 3,000 times, there is not a lot of scope for thinking that there is no energy gain!

9. Another motionless device comes from Tariel Kapanadze from Georgia, in eastern Europe. In one video he demonstrates a self-powered operation with more than 500 watts of continuous 240-volt 50 cycles per second mains output power. He uses two separate Earth connections and starts it operating with a 12V battery. Tariel also has versions with up to 50,000 watts of output. The COP is again infinity as it is self-powered.

10. Another example is James Hardy's (patented) system which uses a high-power water pump to project a jet of water against a paddle wheel, made out of a bicycle wheel with six little cups attached to the wheel which spin the wheel when the water jet hits them. The wheel then turns a shaft which powers a generator, which is connected both to an electric light bulb and to the pump which is powering the system. Output power can be up to 800 watts with the components used in the prototype. Again, the COP is infinity.

11. Another device is shown by Frank Prentice, who used a long wire as an aerial, the kind of wire that runs along a railway line, half a mile to a mile in length. When pulsed with half a kilowatt of electrical signal, it is possible to draw up to 3 Kilowatts of output power from this very simple device

12. I have another friend in Australia called Chas Campbell, his device has an output of 3 Kilowatts, he took a mains motor, driven by 50 cycles per second, 230 Volts mains. He geared it down to drive a series of shafts and a flywheel weighing 20 kilograms. The final output shaft of this device is geared up to an electrical generator and he found that he could make it self-powered and power additional equipment from the generator.

13. A man called Marvin Cole in the USA, built an electric motor which was based on a design by Nikola Tesla. He got the motor independently tested by Cal-Tech. They certified that it had an input requirement of just 27 watts when producing a 10 horsepower output, that is 7.45 kilowatts coming out and a COP of 275.

14. Then there is Richard Willis in Canada. he has a solid state pulsing system. The COP is 3,600, and he is offering 4.8 Kilowatt to 15 Kilowatt units for sale.

15. Thomas Henry Moray, used aerial systems, again pulling the power entirely from the air. He gave many public demonstrations where he cut the wires and placed a piece of glass between the cut ends of the wires and the power kept flowing. He had units with up to 50 kilowatt output. He was shot at repeatedly and eventually intimidated into silence about his methods.

16. For some forty years now, ShengHe Wang of China has been building motors powered only by permanent magnets. He has designs giving 1 kilowatt, 5 kilowatts and 50 kilowatts. He would like to give the design freely to every country in the world so that these motors could be made easily in any country, but he is not allowed to do that. He is a typical inventor with no understanding at all of the economic policies of the opposition.

C - *How can we make these kinds of devices available when we have such resistance from the Oligarchic and Energy Monopolies in countries like the USA and Europe today?*

Patrick - *I would imagine that because the government is taking so much in the way of taxes, that the typical excuse will be that you cannot sell any Free-energy device until it has "passed our safety and reliability certification tests". If an inventor says "well this particular unit has passed China's reliability and safety tests", they would probably just say "Well, it has not passed ours, and we are not China". With methods like that, governments will make sure that such devices will never reach the marketplace.*

More and more Free-Energy devices are emerging all over the world, China is not going along with the repression of Free Energy and it is too large a nation for any other country to do anything about although their free-energy generators are likely to be sold solely within China for some years to come. In America, the privately owned Patent Office is reported to have already managed to suppress some 44,000 American free-energy patents.

It is perfectly possible to run an unmodified electricity generator on HHO gas from water, plus some cold water mist. Many kilowatts of excess electrical power can be produced by that method and these generators have been run like this in remote areas for several years now.

There is an aerial system made by Lawrence Rayburn in Canada. This aerial forms a tuned resonant cavity up to the ionosphere. He was intending to market kits for people to use it and generate 10 Kilowatts of continuous mains power from it, but then, Lawrence decided that it was too dangerous for an untrained person to use safely, and so he does not publicise his design.

Jim Watson built a really massive version of John Bedini's self-powered flywheel system. John's system ran continuously self-powered in his workshop for more than three years. So Jim Watson built a bigger version using the starter motor, for an aircraft. The flywheel was 8 to 10 ft in diameter, the device was 20 ft long, 10 feet wide and 10 feet tall, he showed it at the 1985 TeslaTech Conference, it was charging its own batteries as well as putting out about 12 Kilowatts of excess power. He was intimidated and bought out by the opposition. Threatening the lives of whole families has proved to be very effective in the past.

Although it can happen the other way around – Paul Zigouras of the 'water car' forum produced a system which could blast a jet of water from a hose pipe into HHO gas at an enormous rate capable of powering a 235 HP marine engine, but he implied that he could be bought out. He was paid US $6,000,000 for it, which was the amount he was asking for.

Producing as much as 32 kilowatts from an input of a mere 25 watts, one replication of The Adams Motor is a most impressive performance. A typical Adams Motor designed by Robert Adams of New Zealand, is generally about 8 inches across, being a single rotor with magnets mounted on it and stationary pick-up coils positioned around the rotor. With careful adjustment, even a poorly constructed Adams Motor can be expected to have eight times more output than input.

Moving up to 100 kilowatts or more, Don Smith built a device like a Tesla Coil, operating at high frequency and high voltage. With skilful tuning, many kilowatts of power can be drawn from such a design. However, high voltage components are very expensive and so the device can cost a good deal to make and a lot of time may be needed when searching for the exact components required.

A man called Josef Papp produced 223 kilowatts from an adapted Volvo 90 horse power car engine. He sealed off the intake and exhaust, filled the crank case with a mixture of very pure inert gases, argon, krypton, neon,....He gave an indoor demonstration where he produced a measured 300 horsepower for 35 minutes with literally, no intake, no exhaust and no normal fuel used.

Let's take a look at another inventor who could produce 1.5 Megawatts (1,500 Kilowatts) and who had this device running under test for a period of two years with the only moving part in his system being water which was circulating inside a toroidal pipe. Produced by Dr Oleg Gritskevitch of the USSR, it was a toroid container covered inside with a special barium coating. Then the pipe was filled with highly distilled water. He put a series of electrical winding wires around the torrid and added some pipes with cooling water to keep the temperature down. He started it off with 110,000 Volts, at a sustained 50 milli-watts of current for 3 to 5 minutes. Once started, the water kept moving around and around continuously, and with the electrodes in it, he was able to pull off one and a half Megawatts of power. His workshop was eventually burned down as you can imagine they were not so keen on his invention.

C - *Have you attempted to build or replicate any such devices yourself?*

Patrick - *I have produced one or two of these, but I am not a skilled builder of mechanical devices. Consequently, I prefer electronic things as they don't have to be mechanically perfect in order to function. I once built a Bedini Wheel and we used it in a couple of Seminars in South Wales, we wanted to show the audience that building something like this is straightforward, we had some of the people that came to the seminar help us build the Bedini Pulser Wheel, it was built in about half an hour, then we fired it up and it charged the battery, we used a 20 inch bicycle wheel, 8 magnets and a coil of wire in the centre of the wheel, the circuitry was put together using standard electrical screw connectors.*

I have also made a modified "Joule Thief" circuit for battery charging and proved COP>2 performance by cross-charging two identical lead-acid batteries, both of which ended up with substantially greater usable power, in spite of the fact that the batteries were only 50% efficient and so had to receive twice as much input current as they were then able to supply.

C - *Can you see any of these devices being used in alternative communities in the future?*

Patrick - *Yes, I know of 7 generators being used off the grid in various countries, and some of these have been in use for more than 6 years now. There will be many, many more which I have not heard about.*

C - *Compressed Air Cars have recently emerged in France, what is your opinion on such cars.*

Patrick - *Most compressed air cars are not self-sustaining, there is a patented design by Leroy Rogers which can be fitted to existing cars, and provided that you are going at more than 30 miles an hour, it is actually self-sustaining. Compressed air is a good way to store energy for later use and wind power and solar power could be used to compress air during the day, ready for later use.*

However, you must remember that the people with the most influence today, are the researchers or professors in universities. Generally speaking, these people are controlled by professors whose reputations require the regular publication of research papers from their university. Unfortunately, those research projects are funded by grants which come from people who are rich enough to provide grants, and those are usually people who are part of the opposition to real scientific advancement. They can then use their influence to ensure that no project which they don't approve will ever be funded by them.

If any of the researchers step out of line and campaign for alternative energy, then in order to save their own jobs, all of the other professors will say that such a device or project would be against the laws of physics and in particular, there is no such thing as "perpetual motion". Personally, I don't know of anything in the universe which is not in perpetual motion.

C- *How do you see the next ten years unfolding for Free Energy devices?*

Patrick - *I would see Free Energy Devices becoming available for sale in places like China, Hong Kong, and Eastern Europe. When that happens and people learn about Free Energy devices going on sale there, it raises questions for people living in Europe, UK and countries that are supposed to be a democracy, namely, "how can they have them and we can't?". That is an awkward question to answer if you are the power companies and government when the actual answer is "we don't want you to have these devices, because you pay us more money if you don't have them". Politicians don't like answering questions like that, quite apart from not liking to answer questions in general.*

However, the information available on the internet makes it difficult to suppress this information especially the videos on YouTube of devices already operating. They will try to suppress it as much as possible for a while but the process of trying to censor the internet at this point is challenging. One way of censoring such information is under the guise of anti-terrorism and under the guise of suppressing paedophiles, in order to close down any sites which they don't like and which could be a threat to their power. Basically, that is, any sites criticising the government, they will attempt to close down or censor under the guise that they are websites spreading subversive information which would include Free-Energy websites. If they succeed in censoring sites to such a degree, it will just push us back to using bulletin boards or some form of peer to peer community networks, and self-publishing on paper.

The biggest challenge that any Free Energy inventor has, is marketing their device, as it is nearly impossible, considering the people who oppose that happening. Take Cal-Tech again as an example. They developed a carburettor that allowed a car to run for 150 miles per US gallon, and with no pollution. After successful testing they associated with a company Arvin Meritor to market it, and as soon as they did, that company was bought out by 'One Equity Partners' and the section dealing with Cal-Tech was closed down. The Cal-Tech carburettor never reached the market in spite of Caltech having spent a million dollars developing this product.

On a positive note going back to China, South Africa and Eastern Europe again, that is where Free-Energy products will first be used to power industry and then domestic needs, but bringing such devices to the UK and America will be difficult.

ENDNOTES: Chapter 7

1. EPIA Global Solar Photovoltaic Report. Global Market Outlook for Photovoltaic - epia.org/

2. Patrick Kelly's Free Energy Website free-energy-info.co.uk

3 Over Unity Forum. overunity.com

4. Shell Oil Profit- Comparing British BP with Shell Oil profits- www.iii.co.uk/articles/182699/shell-vs-bp-who-wins

5. Sierra Club (March, 2014) *Polluting our Democracy and our Environment.* -

6. Nafeez Ahmed. *How Blair's Egyptian gas gambit advances the Israeli energy empire*. Saturday 14 March 2015. Middle East Eye. -

7. Scott Brusaw. Ted Talks. The Promise of Solar Roads- Available online

8. Eindhoven Solar Car- solarteameindhoven.nl

9. Stanley Meyer, Water car Patent- peswiki.com/index.php/Directory:Stanley_Meyer

10. Robert Lee. Water Powered Car Hits Mainstream in Pakistan. Pure Energy Systems News. Peswiki. 28th June, 2012

11. Genepax Japan genepax.com

12. Compressed Air Cars- mdi.lu

13. Paramahamsa Tewari - *Nuclear engineer out to rewrite laws of physics.* Feb 12th, 2002. Times of India,

14. The original Patrick Kelly Interview with the author, which the transcript is based on can be listened to here online : sailingbeyondknowledge.wordpress.com/2010/06/04/scratching-the-surface-of-free-energy-devices-with-patrick-kelly/

Chapter 8: The Perspective of a Free Energy Inventor

[1]Sir John Searl – Free Energy Inventor Interview. 20th May, 2011.

I was very honoured and graced with the presence of Sir John Roy Robert Searl, a Free-Energy inventor and Bradley Lockerman, the director and producer of "The John Searl Story". Professor Searl has devoted his life to The Searl-Effect Generator, which could solve so many of humanity's energy demands in addition to planet Earth's ecological issues. Professor Searl shares his experiences, challenges and triumphs with the evolution of his work and knowledge of the SEG and how this technology powered by a magnetic generator could be used to transform human society into a sustainable one. John Searl talks about his inspiration and visions in childhood dreams that motivated his building of the SEG, he shares his extraordinary discoveries with the properties which the SEG shows during flight, how it can clean up radiation, transform seawater into fresh pure drinking water, the SEG also addresses drought and could provide rain where there are deserts, and provides incredible benefits to human health. Bradley Lockerman highlights that NASA's latest findings on dark energy, can explain the physics behind the Inverse Gravity Vehicle (the levitation disc) which enables it to fly so efficiently. John Searl explains how the SEG flight model could provide fast economic and safe air transportation in minutes rather than hours from continent to continent and that it could be used as a more efficient securer form of space travel. The uses and benefits of the SEG are limitless and the science and technology it could provide humanity is fascinating and enlightening. Professor Searl has devoted his entire life to making the SEG available to transform humanity to become more sustainable on planet Earth.

''All truth passes through three stages. First, it is ridiculed. Second, it is violently opposed. Third, it is accepted as being self-evident'' - Arthur Schopenhauer.

The Pentagon spends US $82 million each day with no public transparency to where this money is going. Every minute of every day, oil companies make millions of dollars in profit. Oil companies such as Exxon earn US $390 billion in revenue and a profit of US $170 billion increasing each year, this is why oil companies can buy seats in political parties, which are a tactical move to further protect profit avenues and keep out developments of sustainable technologies which would threaten their current profits. Five percent of the Earth's population, living in the USA, uses 25 percent of the world's oil. Oil consumption is expected to increase to 120 million barrels per day by 2020. Is there really an economic collapse or is the economic collapse due to misspending and lack of public transparency in government spending? Trillions of US dollars has been spent on war, on nuclear power, on oil, where is the money to be spent on alternative energy solutions, holistic health care, education and clean water access, after two recent major environmental disasters, the gulf oil disaster and the Fukushima nuclear disaster both should demonstrate that we have invested far too much faith in destructive energy methods, we need to move away from these environmentally destructive forms of energy production.

Sir John Searl is an inventor from the UK, a pioneer in anti-gravity and Free-Energy inventions. Professor Searl's SEG device could provide solutions to many of humanity's problems in transport and alternative clean energy production. The Searl Effect Generator promises to be one of mankind's greatest inventions and a window to new possibilities, like many other Free Energy devices, however it continues to be conveniently ignored. Professor Searl's desire is to see this device implemented for the benefit of humankind and the environment. The story of his hardships and persecution is a long one, it is amazing that he is still alive today and in his retirement. He has resisted being bought out by energy companies and has survived persecution from pathological sceptics deployed to discredit alternative energy inventors and so protect the profits of the oil giants.

Governments only fund science institutions or academic departments which run projects to support the government agendas, they will never knowingly fund a project that endangers their economic profits.

Sir John Searl came from very humble beginnings; he was brought up in a care home as he was not treated very well by his parents. He had the added challenge of having to deal with deafness since early childhood and as a child he wasn't treated very well by his peers. The following information is from a first-hand interview between me and Sir John Searl.

Searl: "*When I was a child I had a set of dreams that set me on my journey to building the SEG device. The first dream was of me going to school and playing a game similar to hopscotch before arriving at school. The second dream relates to what I did when I arrived home from school. Making sure the hens were bedded down for the night with fresh straw*".

The meaning and symbology in these dreams which he goes into more detail about later gave him the information that led him to build the first device which he made. He goes on to explain how the law of squares relates to his dreams, for example the hopscotch game kept appearing in his dreams twice a year for six years. I asked him what is the significance of the law of squares,

Searl: *I discovered an error of teaching in the Law of Squares, this was indicated through the repetitive hopscotch dreams, I can do the Law of Squares really quickly, there are two key people that contributed to knowledge in normal engineering. The first is Sir Isaac Newton and if a project doesn't work according to Newton's assumptions which are called "laws", we then turn to Einstein, so between these two people the project which you're developing will work. However with the Law of Squares, there are no two different states, it works for everything.*

Searl has written a book on the Law of Squares, one of over a hundred books, and two hundred news articles. He was aged fourteen years old when he started building a domestic generator. That particular device inverted gravity and converted it into a repelling force, which when encountering the Earth's gravity, gets pushed back.

C: *Why did you specifically use rare-earth, Neodymium in your devices and do you know why it has the special properties it has to produce excess electrons, why they were replenished easily or was it something which you were already aware of before choosing the elements or was it something you encountered during the process of experimenting with materials?*

Searl: *Well, to be honest I knew nothing about elements. All I knew was the dreams, the steps of the dreams and taking those steps, element 60 was the figure I came to, when I checked it on the elements chart it was Neodymium. At that time it was only used by glass manufacturers. They polished glass with it and used it to colour the glass purple, which was all it was used for at that time. So because the dream suggested element 60, I ordered it and I'd like people to know that in 1946, a kilo of rare earth element cost only 32 pence per kilo. Now it costs 35 pounds plus sales tax for just 5 grams, so now we are talking about thousands of pounds to produce a plate of that material.*

C: *Why does it cost so much today?*

Searl: *China has already stated that they will not supply that rare-earth element to buyers outside China. It is not that it is in short supply, but the demand for it is so high. We can use other rare earth elements in place of this material, what makes them special is that they have the ability to hold an extra band of electrons in that element, which is a beautiful thing for this SEG technology to kick-start the system.*

C: *Going on to what you have probably dealt with the most in your life: the response of most incredulous sceptics who cannot wrap their brains around, is that your work and the work of other Free-Energy Inventors proves that there is an unseen energy field which mainstream physics has continuously negated, while Nikola Tesla, Wilhelm Reich and Henrich Casimir discoveries have clearly demonstrated this fact. Today we still have much to learn, and most people's understanding of magnets and magnetism is pretty basic, in terms of understanding the polarities of North and South. Could you please share the discoveries you made in your life's work on how magnetic forces behave in your own levitation disc, with detail on* *what you learned on the diverse spectrum of the magnetic sine waves that you personally witnessed?*

Searl: *Well first of all, I accepted that the electron, light and magnetism were all the same thing, viewed from different dimensions, therefore if magnetism was the same as light, light we accept has several different bands of frequencies due to different bands of colour, now each colour has a magnetic field to it and therefore, I was looking at ways, in which we could produce a particular magnetic field from a light band, that would produce the magnetic field that we want, that is a wave, and not just straight poles as in common magnets. We found that we were able to do it, and if we followed the Laws of Squares values we could produce a generator, in fact it really is a converter, that takes energy from around the room and sucks it in, compresses it and puts it out as useful energy. You will notice that the temperature drops around the machine, because you are compressing electrons, and therefore they haven't got so much room between them to build up energy when they hit another electron to release that energy and make heat. Therefore we have a machine that runs cool, and if you are not careful it will run very cool and take off.*

C: *That is interesting as it ties into the next question. In Bradley Lockerman's documentary of your work, John Thomas talks about how the generator drops to 4 degrees Kelvin which results in the effect called 'cold numbing', and that, he explains is a result of superconductivity and anti-gravity so in the film there is an animation that shows a toroidal type energy field expanding exponentially around the SEG device. So would you explain a bit about how this works in terms of creating the force field for the flight of your levitation discs.*

Searl: *Well the flight of what was called the levitation disc are now termed 'inverse gravity vehicles'. First of all, the superconductivity state causes it to rise, then we have the vortex effect above the craft, which is pulling the rolling magnets that are spinning around, causing the air to pull towards them, because these rollers are in rotation the air rotates, therefore we have a suction effect above the vehicle, then underneath the air is rushing in through a gap which* *creates more push underneath and the suction above, so the craft flies up with very little effort, but it takes a bit more effort to bring it down to the ground again.*

C: *The first time you discovered that your device could fly was when you explained how it took off at your home in the kitchen of Crawley Road. When you discovered this, it must have been a really shocking moment for you would you share with us what happened?*

Searl: *Nowhere in physics does it ever state what happens when you fool around with magnetism, nor does it say that a magnetic device would go up in the air with the force behind it to push it up in the air, therefore, I thought it was quite safe to make this generator which I was dreaming of. I told the landlady what I was doing, and she asked me, "it won't blow the fuses will it?" I assured her "no, no, it is quite okay", so we plugged it in and of course within seconds, it tore away and rushed to the ceiling and just hung there, and I remarked, 'that is a silly thing, what is it doing up there? It should be on the table!' We had to get the step ladder and I asked her to help me because when I grabbed the bars inside the vehicle to pull it down, my hands were stuck frozen to it, and I had to ask the landlady if she could come up and bring a screwdriver to ram it inside and stop the magnetic rollers from turning, which she did, it then came down, then she had to bring some hot water to pour over the handles to get my hands unstuck. It was quite a shock, as everyone was telling me, it could not happen it was impossible and here it was happening.*

I had a question, how am I going to stop the levitation disc lifting off the table, so I put a lead plate underneath, was that the solution? No, I made a right cock-up there, as it was worse. It now went through the ceiling and out through the roof, and hovered there, not only that but it was sending out an electrical static field, and we only had long wave radio in those days, which meant we had to run a long copper wire out down to the garden to pick up the station signals, and of course the static hit those wires, came in and jumped the capacitor at the back of the aerial, and the volume was at maximum, so I guess I could say I wasn't a very popular man after that in the neighbourhood, because no one could turn their radio sets on until the levitation disc flew away, and it all went dead.

That wasn't all. At that time, I was staying with an old man called George Hayes. He was dying of cancer and he was a great listener to the radio program devoted to the Pope's 8 o'clock message, and I would sit beside him as a companion while he listened to the radio and after he said to me, John what is your interest, and I told him about this levitation disc, and the flying machine, and he said to me "John if you can make people look up into the sky, I will pay the price to do it, because everyone walks with their head down. So he asked his son to take me to the market that week to buy all the bits and pieces that I needed. I built it and of course it had the same effect when I launched the first one went above the tree tops and hovered, then the power came on the radio sets and fled away and disappeared, after I went up to the old man and told him I am sorry we've lost it. He said "John, did they look up?" I said yes, everybody came out of their doors to see what was happening because of the noise on their radio sets. The old man then replied, "then build another one", so we built another one, but this time we suggested that we'd tether it to make sure that it did not shoot away, that we did, but eventually it still broke away, of course with all the upsets again, by the time we built the forth one, an airman was on holiday staying in the house opposite, he came out and started shooting a gun at me, so the police came, and he told the police that I was frightening his pigeons. What he meant was that the pigeons were unloading their waste quicker and he didn't like the job of cleaning it up.

Through my life I look at all the problems, I must admit I was a bit of a naughty boy at times, I would let the craft fly over the roof tops of houses and make the tiles rattle, that used to frighten people and of course even in the day time I'd wait at a bend in the road, and wait for cars to come along, then send it out and people in their cars would react when they saw it hovering in front of them, they would put their car in reverse gear from the main road, I couldn't understand how those gears could stand the wear, everyone had the same reaction. One day returning from Warminster to Newbury, there is a nice sloped hill on our left side as we drove towards

Newbury and down this hill was a lot of sheep, following a tractor with a trailer, but there was no driver on the seat of the tractor, so we were looking to see where he was and he was along the side of the trailer with a fork lifting the straw off and spreading it around for the sheep. So I thought on a nice sunny day, I will have a little bit of fun here, so I sent the vehicle up in a big loop behind him so he wouldn't see it until eventually it flew over him and he could see its dark shadow cast on the ground while he was pitch-forking the straw out on to the ground. I wondered how long it would be before he would look up, eventually he looks up and saw the disc hovering there, but instead of getting into the running tractor, he leaves the tractor and runs in the other way up the hill. The only thing I was sorry for, was that I did not have a camera at the other end to explain what had happened to his tractor, I do know it was saved as it ran into a ditch. I decided after that to relocate to another area before unusual visitors popped up looking for aliens.

C: *So it was some years before you started building these discs when you met Mr Haynes. Would you tell us how many you built altogether and what some of the challenges were?*

Above pictures of Searl's levitation discs test flights.

Searl: *Well, altogether there were forty one vehicles built, what we wanted to do was after each one passed all we wanted to know and* *test, we just opened it up and then enlarged it, which saved money. The SEG part is a plate made in segments, so it wasn't difficult to make another segment to fit in and enlarge it. The backers that were supporting us, most had died, there were only a few people left, and they couldn't afford to continue supporting us, so I had to call an end to that. That was when we started to work on a man craft version.*

C: *You had some issues controlling the discs first of all, is that right?*

Searl: *You couldn't control these discs with a normal model radio control system. You had to use ham operators. We found plenty of volunteers willing to join the team to do that. So we were able to send the craft anywhere we wanted to.*

C: *Could you explain what a Ham radio operator was as many young people won't be familiar with that term.*

Searl: *Ham operators are people who'd transmit on the radio waves to other people all around the world, they're like a club that is why I was able to talk to friends in Russia and build great friendships, during the cold war there wasn't much difference between the prices in the UK or Russia at that time. The kinds of houses they had there at that time depended on their skill, the more skills you had the better the house you had, it was slightly different to the way we ran the selection of houses for people in the UK, we exchanged basic information.*

C: *What was the longest recorded journey of your levity discs?*

Searl: *Normally what we did was launch a craft on a Sunday evening, then it would be airborne till the following Sunday when it would return, then we would take out the charts that recorded everything that happened on board then examined them. The findings were, based on that, and we were able to move forward. Every model that had been made, actually travelled around the world, each one had done a full test before we decided to make it larger, to find out the advantages gained by being a larger vehicle. One was recorded to go around the Earth 500 times. Of course, the* *larger you make the levitation disc the more economics it requires but it would be able to carry more goods. The main objective of the levitation disc was first as an emergency vessel that could move very quickly to any area in the world, for example it took twenty minutes to travel from New York to London. In the case of a natural disaster such as an earthquake or volcano, to move thousands of people at one time and it could land anywhere where cars and trucks and other land vehicles could not go.*

The second objective is that there was never a problem with volcano ash that other aircraft have. So we could move anywhere in storms, the levitation disc could pass through any storm with no problem, we also discovered that the levitation disc would affect the water content of a storm, it could meet a storm out at sea and break it up before it caused flood damage in a particular area.

C: *That is very interesting as it connects with the work of Trevor James Constable's Rain-engineering where he uses the aetheric forces to break up and dissipate a storm or create rain in areas where there are deserts.*

Searl: *Everyone is concerned about the nuclear fallout over Fukushima. A large SEG over that area could control that problem, the gases that are rising in the air with highly radioactive problems attached to it, the SEG can neutralise radioactivity at the base, we could insert enough electrons so that the neutrons would be pumping back to help stabilise the situation, therefore we would not have so much radiation leaving it to become spread around the Earth.*

The air pollution could also be cleaned up with an SEG, there is a lot of things we could do with these craft, the technology is available and the know-how, it is just the money that has not been put forward to achieve this success.

C: *That is amazing. Going back to what you said earlier about the longest recorded levitation disc journey, did you say that one went around the Earth 500 times?*

Searl: *Yes, that was the last journey we did before we decided to work on a man-sized version. We found that it was possible to direct the craft around this planet to wherever we wanted it to go, we could even have directed it to the moon if we wanted to, therefore, we could direct it to the International Space Station, had it been orbiting. Although it takes the USA a long time to get rockets to the space station, with an levitation disc that is just a bus ride away, it could be achieved within the hour under all conditions, any time, any day, a rocket cannot do that! The weather must be precise for both the leaving and the return journey. This is the difference between a rocket and the levitation disc.*

C: *Your initial objective with these craft was to provide clean and rapid transport for people and for emergency evacuation transport. Do you feel this is overlooked by the press media and public? What kind of reception were you met with in reality at the time when you were working on many different flight models?*

Searl: *The first problem I met was that when I wrote to every car manufacturer about using this SEG technology. They wrote back to say they did not believe that magnetic systems could be built to run a car in our century. They have a lot of money and investments in petrol, so clearly they would not change to another system that did not require petrol or oil at all. That was the problem. Today they might see that they made a terrible mistake with pressure from the government to clean up pollution, it is costing oil companies a fortune to do that, whereby had they spent money on the levitation disc then in 1968, we would have vehicles running on the levitation disc system without any pollution problems. If car manufacturers are looking at producing more electric cars, then surely the sensible way would be to develop the SEG for their driving purposes. Why they have to keep changing these big costly batteries, every two and a half years, where an SEG would just keep running and all you need to worry about is changing the body of the car when you get fed up with the body shape. With an SEG you don't need to worry about wet plugs, over-cooling or over-heating, you can change the temperature quickly and you don't have to wait for the heat, you turn the key on, the electric motors on the wheel and away you go waving* *bye-bye to the Petrol stations, on your way to anywhere you want to go in the world.*

C: *In your opinion, how do you feel that we can break away from the centralisation and monopoly of energy by government and oil companies' controlled economy which also has a tight control over mainstream media.*

Searl: *Governments have to collect their taxes, I appreciate that, it means that if you don't have to buy petrol and oil, you don't pay those taxes. We could surely work together and make this planet a better place for everyone, therefore we would not need to collect masses of taxes from people to survive and we do not see the benefits of this. Tax money is just wasted instead of improving things for us. What we need to do here is change our attitudes and look at our problems and all get together and say 'right, we have some problems here, we are going to have heavy flooding here if we get a severe storm, cut out wider ditches, clean up the rubbish, tidy up the place and by using an SEG we could recover the damage done. The SEG is a golden egg. It can run anything you want to run, you can design it for anything, therefore it is beautiful. But the SEG cannot dig your rubbish out of rivers and oceans for you that is something you need to take responsibility for creating in the first place. What it can do is clean the water. However, we all need to take responsibility and stop creating pollution. The SEG can also enhance human health which is also vital'.*

C: *Most people understand that devices such as the SEG is a major threat to the energy monopolies in oil and nuclear fuel industries. What is your perspective on this?*

Searl: *Whatever they try to do, we have to make changes or perish, there is no other option. What people don't realise, is that with every man who is worried about losing his current job in the current system, the SEG creates ten jobs for every existing job.*

C: *With all that you have shared how do you feel that your work has been suppressed?*

Searl: *Everything I do and work towards is really for the benefit of the planet to create a better world to live in for people and their future children, a cleaner world, a cheaper world with faster transportation that is safe and also to turn deserts into useful land, making Earth into a paradise.*

C: *In comparison to the past, do you feel that your work is being met with a better attitude today or do you think people are not ready to use this technology despite the fact it is a good solution to the current ecological crisis?*

Bradly (documentary film maker on Searl's SEG): *I will jump on that first with a great big 'yes'. Attitudes are changing, the dynamic is changing, the paradigm is changing whether we like it or not. The results which we are getting are more positive these days than they ever have been. John Searl's thoughts and concepts are being accepted in continents all over planet Earth. People who don't even speak English have asked to see the film and want to know who he is, know what he is doing and where he is. So, yes there is a breakthrough coming and a dynamic change, a paradigm change, and it's a choice for those people that see this as we either adapt and change and try things like John Searl's ideas, or we continue down this road which pretty much everyone now assumes is going to be the bad road. There is a shift in thinking. Would you agree John?*

Searl: *Well yes, looking at the internet we see the navy, army and air force, and government officials looking at our website*

Bradley: *The obvious thing is there is a set of individuals, who apparently are not governed by the same set of laws that we are, John was with us earlier this year and he too has seen in America a change in attitudes. There is a cadre of persons throughout the world who have a different set of laws applied to them, it is as if they can bypass the law and allow for their decisions whether legal or not. A little period of time goes by and they'll go back to what they were doing before.*

Going back to the science, something interesting from NASA caught my attention yesterday. The dark energy, constant force in the universe is that which is propelling the universe to accelerate away from itself. Now this is interesting, as Dark Energy is a direct contradiction of Einstein's theory of relativity and so suddenly, theoretically the old standard theories that everyone was bound to, are suddenly being turned on themselves, what does this mean with something like the Searl technology, ideas and concepts? Maybe it means that there is more to this science than people from the past care to acknowledge. So the press release on Dark Energy albeit still in theory, it is as if these people are moving towards Searl's concepts and not the other way around. It is not as great an effort for us to reach out to the pedigree people and I say that with due respect, those people with physics degrees and advanced degrees in science, I have always invited them and I invite them now to come and talk with us, to talk with John Searl and to tell us if they can, where Searl is going wrong? But one question is, if it is true what is currently being investigated regarding Dark Energy, Einstein's theory of gravity is perhaps wrong? That gravity becomes repulsive, instead of attractive, when acting at great distances. If this is being acknowledged by current scientists, this actually agrees with Searl's ideas and technology. John can you verify that?

Sir John Searl's SEG demonstration model

Searl: *Yes, it does. I have disagreed with a number of things that have been classed as 'laws'. Sir Isaac Newton, never stated in his diary that they were laws, they were assumptions, ninety percent of the time he was right but ten percent of the time he was wrong, it doesn't work. Einstein then comes along and fills that gap as his work went further, however, we have to bear in mind the era in which these people lived and what did we know then? They were basing everything on what was known, and what they could perceive, and sometimes when we perceive things, it doesn't happen in the time we think it will happen, it happens much later in time.*

Bradley: *I just want to add and explain a bit more about that article which I read. 'Dark Energy' is the name given to an unexplained force, that is drawing galaxies away from each other, against the pull of gravity, and doing it at an accelerated pace, so dark energy is like anti-gravity and these words are an anathema in physics whereas dark energy tugs them apart on a grander scale. The action of dark energy is as if you threw a ball up in the air and it keeps* *speeding upwards into the sky, constantly gaining speed. Now, suddenly, Dark Energy is a stronger theory than Einstein's theories regarding gravity, and that is just stunning and this paper came out from NASA! Now this plays into what John Searl has been saying for sixty years.*

The existence of Dark Energy is not proven, it is a term used by scientists best guess as to the confusing observation of the universe as expansion is speeding up.

C: *Are you familiar with the book Energy Solution Revolution by Brian O'Leary?*

Bradley: *Yes, I am familiar with O' Leary's work.*

C: *In an earlier interview I did with Sir Trevor James Constable, whom is a pioneer in aetheric rain-engineering, we learned of the unseen aetheric forces that are completely ignored by conventional academic science. These aetheric energies are connected with what is called 'orgone energy', 'chi energy', 'Kundalini energy', 'life force', or 'aether energies' by Gunther Watchsmooth in 1932, in a book called Nature and Cause of the Earth's rotation from the aetheric forces in the cosmos, Earth and man. Wilhelm Reich used the name 'orgone' to explain this energy as the blue energy he saw in his experiments, which is what the ancient Chinese medical scientists call chi energy as far back as eight thousand years ago, which is the same energy that runs through the Earth as ley lines, which is the healing energy that Van Tassle tuned into with his Integratron dome building which he built to rejuvenate human cells and prolong human health and vitality. It is noted in a lot of research on different types of free-energy devices, but most have one thing in common other than just generating a far greater output of energy than what goes in. That commonality is many devices including the ones Searl has made, Searl himself has claimed that his devices are beneficial to human health. Many devices made by different Free-Energy scientists have been noted promote general human health along with plant health and animal health. It is as if some of the devices that can do this as a by-product of producing free energy are tapping into the ether to promote further orgone or chi or aetheric* *forces that are healing to all living beings. Is it not therefore an example in itself, why we need to start tuning in and resonating with Earth's aetheric forces as explained by Watchsmooth, Trevor James Constable, Wilhelm Reich, and Rudolph Steiner.*

Searl: *When you are seated beside an SEG and breathing, it's not like you are breathing but like you are drinking in fresh clean spring water because it cleans the air, it literally sanitises it from germs and bacteria because it negatively ionises the air. I had a lot of energy when I worked on these devices, I could work non-stop day and night around one as I felt good. The SEG can also purify water. Working with water is really easy because it is a polarised molecule. An SEG is a golden egg because you could convert tons of sea water into fresh drinking water. There is no need to say that there is a shortage of water, all we have to do is purify it. In terms of other useful features, look at radiation energy, and the SEG as a converter of wasteful energy into useful energy, so as the SEG sucks in air, it can be converted into electrical energy, then when you release it, it does the job and goes back to what it was. It is like a waterwheel system, you have a big reservoir of water and control the down-feed to the wheel and as it falls to the wheel, it gathers kinetic energy , when it hits the wheel , it is the kinetic energy in the water that causes it to turn, and the water continues the way it was going.*

For the energy you could turn an axle that turns a generator that produces power to run all the machinery. A few years back, I was explaining this on TV about the levitation disc that the energy goes out as photons when they do go back together, it is as electrons which then find their way to the shell of the craft (SEG). The response was that 'no work was done', so what they are saying to me is the water comes down, you turn the wheel and if you have an electric pump on it, that pumps the water back to the reservoir, 'no work was done', so all those metal sheets with holes in them, suddenly have no holes in them, the holes are there because the work was done. We returned the water to the reservoir because we haven't damaged the water. The same analogy applies to the electrons - we pass them back to the air again because we haven't damaged them.

Bradley: *Yes this is one of the arguments we think we have been able to overcome and that is of course entropy, nothing can be created or destroyed, a lot of people don't understand that in the Searl converter, nothing is created or destroyed, so those electrons that are passing through the system are not created or destroyed, they pass through and were compressed, used and restored. Isn't that correct John?*

Searl : *Yes!*

C: *That leads on to my next question, because the Searl Effect Generator has come to being looked on by the Free-Energy community as an example of Schopenhauer's transition to truth! As we discuss mainstream media and academic science, refuse to acknowledge specific unseen energy sources which makes it difficult for new energy scientists such as yourself to convince those incredulous sceptics, to the need for us to reconsider and rewrite the laws and assumptions of physics, which are just theories after all anyway, such as the big bang, thermodynamics and dark energy as your example Bradley, where you shared new information on that. Would you explain what kind of implications this has caused your work John and your objectives in making the SEG available to humankind?*

Searl: *We were compressing wasted energy which was hot, which then becomes cold, by the simple fact that the electrons themselves have very little room to move about, so they build up this great release of energy where they have much more space, therefore we are harnessing the energy and matter saturation, so we are conserving energy.*

Bradley: *John, in reference to the theories that are present today, as those theories are crumbling, they are coming closer to your way of thinking?*

Searl: *That is without a doubt! What they are saying now, is basically what I have been saying all these years, but because it is based on their teachings, as they do not take my research and technology seriously.*

C: *That is the issue we have with mainstream science being funded by the oligarchy, biased to only support the work of scientists that produce work which upholds the oligarchic agenda. What has happened to your SEG generators? Are there any left?*

Searl: *There is one floating around somewhere, another was dumped on a rubbish heap by the council , it was part of belongings left behind by a friend who died and who had no relatives and no one to whom to leave his things, so the council cleared out his apartment, so that one has been destroyed. There is another around somewhere, I believe the man is still alive. He was given a month left to live so he bought one of my devices to help invigorate his health and yes he is still about to this day. The others I had that Reverend George Nixon returned to me, and one I had left were destroyed by the authorities for the reasons that it did not conform to their rules and regulations.*

The original SEG took three months to make, it was for research and studies and not for commercial use. Since 1968, I have made several attempts to go commercial. Since then, it has been challenging, we reach the top of the hill, team members stole all the equipment, thinking everything was on the computers, so they could make the SEG for nothing. There are still people we come up against today who are determined to stop this technology getting to the marketplace, because we won't allow them to own it.

C: *It is a threat to the central energy cartel. What are your current plans for building a new SEG and what are the costs involved with building one?*

Searl: *Now we have our own site to build a device, thanks to people whom donated to give support, before we had used other people's land and unfortunately they would tell us to leave once they thought they knew how to build our devices and they took everything, this happened in Thailand which Bradley Lockerman knows about. The magnetic development and engineering of the work has to be kept separate from the rest of the work because if we allow people to know how to make the magnetisers, if they were used for malevolent causes, they could wipe a city's electrical grid out, through towns* *and set up the magnetisers letting the waves go wild, so all electrical devices within that field would be rendered useless. We now only employ engineers who have a certain level of security clearance that will allow them to work in the presence of the director's office while he is there. That is the type of security we need now, to avoid this technology getting into the wrong hands.*

C: *Sometimes the wrong hands can be the government's hands!*

Searl: *Yes, this is why we endeavour to keep this technology as a project by the people for the people, I have always invited government officials, military and the like to come and have a cup of tea and a chat and see for themselves, I have nothing to hide, everything I do is for the benefit of people and the planet. We have a lot of promises, for example investors contact us and say they will put a few million in the bank account but that never happens, and they continue to make the same promises several weeks later.*

Bradley: *Quite true, John was here a few weeks ago and we were entertaining a representative from a well-known aircraft company. It was very amusing to see how perplexed he was, to see him keep looking at the SEG mock up, starring and scratching his head. The mock up demonstrates several things, a principle that is so obvious and so simple. This confounded an aspect for the representative with the question, not what was it doing but can it be that simple? John what would you say?*

Searl: *Yes, what I noticed was that he was concerned about the hole in the plate, he couldn't accept that if nothing was put in the centre hole, that it wouldn't work. The revolving rollers go around at speed around a ring, and we could prove with just that alone, it took very low voltage withdrawn from the plate to make the rollers run.*

Bradley: *The key thing here is that in the mock up set up we were inducing a 3V to 7V voltage from the centre to the rim, however that is replaced by the kick-start of the Neodymium spare electrons which is the most interesting thing about the mock up, would you say that is true John?*

Searl: *That is correct, we are not using that rare earth in the mock up, and we needed to find out what was the energy that made those rollers move, to see if the rare earth was providing the energy to make them move without any input from other sources.*

Bradley: *And John, when we were back at Middlesex University, you were able to establish a static charge of 7 volts, is that correct?*

Searl: *On the British version we had 3.5 volts, on the German version we had 15 volts.*

Bradley: *Now, keep in mind what that means. When you are looking at the mock-up, we are using a transformer to substitute for the Neodymium, well, remove that and put the Neodymium in, and you have that 3.5 up to 15 volts, it is there so let's use it!*

Searl: *Just to clarify that is per segment, there are eight segments of rollers, there are twelve rollers on the first one, and twenty two on the next layer of rollers, and that plate which we tested, gave one hundred volts to six hundred volts on one lead contact only, with two lead contacts it gave an output of three and a half thousand volts coming from the first plate alone, on top of that there are two bigger plates that complete the whole SEG. The amount of power produced that comes off that final plate is unbelievable.*

Bradley: *To add to what Sir John just said, that is similar to a capacitor or transistor, is that true John?*

Searl: *It operates the same as a giant transistor in concept.*

C: *Have you ever met Dr Stephen Greer and his involvement with the Disclosure Project? I am surprised that in all the talks he has done, he has never referred to your work and I discussed this with Jason Verbelli the other day and he told me that he confronted Greer about you as apparently Greer did say that he met you once and that you showed him a device and Jason said this was not true.*

Bradley: *I support their intentions, I am surprised that they have not taken an interest in what John is doing, where he is and what we* *have happening on our projects here. Disclosure is a very important thing and while John Searl was visiting us here in the States. If any of the security people are hiding and observing us, we would like to invite them in and talk with us, quit hiding for heaven's sake.*

C: *Is there anything else you would like to add regarding implications of marketing and getting your SEG device available for domestic and industrial context?*

Bradley: *It is up to our organisational capacity, infrastructure and our ability to produce something in an R and D facility, that is exactly what we have done, and exactly what we have set up, ideally we would like to have John Searl himself, nearby to be able to come to the lab daily, to help us towards that effort, his main function of course is to continue writing the books and to continue informing people about what we are doing step by step. It is really a recreation step by step in terms of infrastructure and business plans. We are ready to go, one of the big hold ups, which I think John mentioned earlier, is that in the old days, he would use a slurry mixture, in order to make the component parts. His idea now is to have a system that can be replicated in much less time and effort than previously. We are trying to do this at the facility, the layered elements that can be removed from the facility into mass production instantly upon achievement of our ultimate goal which is the working ring and roller set of the SEG. Is that correct John?*

Searl: *That is correct.*

C: *How would you like to see the future of the SEG?*

Searl: *I want to see the SEG used to power hospitals, saving them a vast amount in energy costs, and therefore they can now pay better wages to the hospital staff. I'd like to see the SEG available to people in domestic settings and individual power systems. I'd like to see every form of modern transport running using the SEG technology. I' d like to see a commercial space program, not government controlled, to investigate space using the SEG technology to seek out materials that would benefit our* *manufacturing plant, instead of destroying the Earth to get the raw materials.*

Bradley: *John and I had a meeting when he was visiting here in Los Angeles over at the veterans meeting, and they brought up a very interesting point regarding hospitals using the SEG technology as opposed to being on the grid, if they were in the middle of an operation, something severe or any of the medical equipment in the intensive care units, were to have a power failure, what kind of liabilities do hospitals or medical staff face under such conditions which of course is through no fault of theirs, but the litigation and liability of losing power at a critical moment in such health facilities would be just staggering.*

Searl: *Yes, with an SEG, it would continue to run and probably outlive the building structure and become the eighth wonder of the world, joining the Great Pyramids and other wonders of the world. The Pyramids were built by a nation and we are still arguing about how they did it. Let us hope that future generations do not wonder at how we could turn deserts green. How we could reduce illnesses and pollution in the air and oceans, how we improve our food quality. We want to leave records of precisely how and who did it. We can, we have the know-how, we have the technology, what we need is the finances and you people out there supporting us to make it happen, it requires people to get involved to make those changes. We can do it, if they could build pyramids in ancient times, we can turn deserts green. It is up to you, if you want a better life, a happier life, a healthier life, and a bright future, but we need your support to accomplish that.*

C: *Bradley would you like to tell us about your journey of making your documentary with John Searl?*

Bradley: *Obviously now people know a bit more about John Searl, he is a charming, likable fellow, his story is off the charts fascinating, I haven't met anyone yet that is not charmed and fascinated by him, as far as making the film it has been a great venture, but I can say this, the best is yet to unfold. Something will happen in the future and it will be stunning.*

Searl: *Thank you very much for putting up with me and I hope that your listeners continue to listen to the program and I wish all of them the best for the future.*

ENDNOTES: Chapter 8

1. Transcript from originally recorded interview between author and Sir John Searl sailingbeyondknowledge.wordpress.com/2011/05/21/episode-42-the-john-searl-effect-solution/
2. Sir John Searl's websites swallowcommand.com/JohnUSA.html and
3. searleffect.com
4. Bradley Lockerman documentary on Sir John Searl
5. johnsearlstory.com

Chapter 9: Ecology of Consciousness

An aspect of Deep Ecology is Eco-psychology or Eco-therapy and it takes into account our internal emotional and mental state and how this is creating our external environment. You may have had feelings of being unfulfilled, deepening apathy, depression, loss, anxiety and despair. Perhaps these feelings are rooted in the belief that we are separate from nature? It is understandable, considering the current world situation. Anyone that is not deeply saddened by current global events are either in denial or very disconnected from the Earth and their true nature. Many of us are going through different stages of this, yet not realising that these are psychological symptoms of the collective unconscious, a reaction to the world in its current state of ecocide (apocalypse). We may think that these feelings of frustration, anger, grief and depression are a reflection of personal problems but they are not, the bigger picture is that these symptoms are indications that something is deeply wrong with modern society. The toxicity and predatory nature of modern capitalism has created these symptoms in our collective unconscious.

Depression is an indication that Human understanding of itself in relation to the natural world, needs to change. Some people refer to depression as a 'disease'. It is not a disease, but more chemical and emotional imbalance of the brain, normally affected by long-term stress, deep trauma or grief, for some it is difficult to diagnose the root cause. [1]Dr John Grohol defines depression for those who insist on calling it a disease.

"*These things are called disorders, not diseases, for a reason. A disorder simply means something that is out of the ordinary, which depression and other mental disorders are. They are more specifically a cluster of symptoms that research has shown to correlate highly with a specific emotional state.*"- Dr Grohol.

Furthermore, should it really be referred to as a 'mental illness' either? Through my research and personal experiences, depression is an understandable psychological reaction to the stress and violent deformities of the modern world.

The most valuable activities that can help, are spending time in nature or in the company of animals, writing and creating and being as honest with one's self or one's true nature. If one doesn't feel in touch with one's true nature, just go with what makes you feel happy, comfortable or what inspires you, even the smallest thing helps point towards your truer nature.

Obviously, getting to the possible triggers and issues of depression help, such as recovering from anger, trauma and grief are signals that point towards the root cause of the problem.

People whom suffer from depression are usually highly aware and sensitive folk who are creatively gifted or perceptive in some way. As a result they are people who find it difficult to feel that they fit anywhere in the forms or archetypes dictated by society - a society that places value on things that are leading humanity and the environment to destruction. People who suffer from depression find it difficult to connect with others on a personal level and mostly they are simply overwhelmed and disheartened by the amount of injustice, destruction, greed, cruelty and abuse that goes on in an increasingly hostile world, so if you know someone who is depressed, the best way to support them is find ways to connect with that person on a deeper level if at all possible or encourage them to do activities with you in nature if they don't like to be alone.

A number of environmental scientists such as [2]Dr Stephan Harding, a deep ecologist, like myself, sees the value in needing to restore our lost connection with Earth and understand that we are all part of one greater consciousness. In an early interview Dr Stephan Harding said *"there is something wrong with you if you are not profoundly saddened or depressed by the state of things at the moment"*.

We are living in the sixth greatest mass extinction. Anthropogenic activity is destroying the oceans, ripping apart the last of the Rainforests and indigenous people, we are seeing the largest scale ecocide unfolding. The amount of torture and abuse that our fellow creatures suffer at our own hands, is just overwhelming, let alone the killing, torturing, abusing and trafficking of men, women and children worldwide, innocent victims of insane wars, exploitation and slavery.

It is important to understand the unconscious psychological impact of the current ensuing chaos on each of us, as we now have the internet and technologies which bring such information into our awareness. Some of the emotions we feel we may not even be conscious of, as they are a collective conscious reaction to a daily external violence and exploitation, which may stir feelings of grief or guilt, especially if we feel inept or feel we are unable to do anything about many of these issues, our severed connection with mother Earth and our lost ancient knowledge of whom we are and where we have come from. The illusion of our separation from nature has created a very ill and absurd world. It is also disturbing that many people are unstirred, almost completely oblivious to what is going on, and just continue about their day as if the world is going to stay as it is forever, while those of us that are acutely aware of what is unfolding around us try to manage our reaction to it.

We have been made to feel nothing more than human commodities by society, we must be obedient and told that our only value in the modern world, is as a good worker and consumer, whose taxes go to destructive exploits that we have no say in, our privacy is invaded in case we act criminally, yet many governments continue to enjoy privacy and operate corruption behind closed doors. Our human rights are being fast eroded and many of us cannot even imagine a different world. It is a challenge to imagine that we can rise above these lower vibrations. The ecological unconscious where our natural feelings of connection to the world of nature and other organisms rest, are connected to what the biologist [3]E.O. Wilson calls 'biophilia'. People who are the opposite of biophilic, are those that prefer the man-made comforts to nature and therefore are 'biophobic.'

[4] "*Biophilic and biophobic tendencies are a marker of culture (Wilson, 1993) and if we take the assumptions made by various commentators (Foucault, 1964; Horwitz, 2002; Rind & Yuill, 2012) that mental health is a product of its culture, the connection is clearer still. The problems of mental health are shown to be*

increasing the world over (Desjarlais et al, 1995), whilst biophilia as a hypothesis can answer this to a degree, it provides many other answers, namely to do with the origin of many of these conditions that we are experiencing.''- Douglas Radmore, (2014).

Biophobia is a result of modern technology and our dependence on urban life. People who live in cities, tend to survive in a bubble of distraction with iPhones, headphones and music on the go, computer games and living amidst shopping malls, motorways and everything at their convenience, where nature is compartmentalised as parks and squares as decoration. Is Biophobia acceptable? [5]David Orr makes a very good argument on this issue, he states;

First, for every "biophobe" others have to do that much more of the work of preserving, caring for, and loving the nature that supports biophobes and biophiliacs alike. Economists call this the "free-rider problem". It arises in every group, committee, or alliance when it is possible for some to receive all of the advantages of membership while doing none of the work necessary to create those advantages. Environmental free riders benefit from the willingness of others to fight for the clean air that they breathe, the clean water that they drink, the preservation of biological diversity that sustains them, and the conservation of the soil that feeds them. But they do not lift a finger to help. Biophobia is not okay because it does not distribute fairly, the work of keeping the Earth or any local place healthy. Biophobia is not okay for the same reason that misanthropy and sociopathy are not okay. Biophobia is not okay because it is the foundation for a politics of domination and exploitation. For our politics to work as they now do, a large number of people must not like any nature that cannot be repackaged and sold back to them. They must be ecologically illiterate and ecologically incompetent, and they must believe that this is not only inevitable but desirable. Furthermore, they must be ignorant of the basis of their dependency. They must come to see their bondage as freedom and their discontents as commercially solvable problems.'' The drift toward a biophobic society, as George Orwell and C. S. Lewis foresaw decades ago, requires the replacement of nature and human nature by technology and the replacement of real democracy by a technological tyranny now looming on the horizon.''-David Orr.

There are still ways in which we can become self-empowered sovereign beings. There are ways in which we can create a more harmonious and sustainable world without predatory capitalism and it's destructive forces, we can create an alternative ecological and local community based capitalism, instead of the current system which is driving a rise in depression and suicide worldwide, the fundamental principle being that we have lost our true value and our spiritual connection with nature. We have lost our feelings of self-worth with loss of contributing to local communities, (it is human nature to desire to connect with a small local community, like one's own tribe or family, as opposed to contributing to society which is not the same) and feeling valued in that way or in ways we can contribute to working with the land or honouring nature in some way, for the life she sustains, for us. Most of all, we have become empty and bored, due to constant external seeking of fulfilment and stimulus. Even the most privileged people among us suffer from depression, this is an obvious testimony to the fact that all the riches in the world will not make us happy. People have forgotten how to look after their inner spirits, such as taking a walk in nature. Communing with nature soothes the soul and mind.

We must begin to redefine our value as human beings, as part of a larger global community that is working towards change in the midst of all this chaos. We can begin to reclaim our connection with the Earth in various ways through growing food communally, rebuilding and re-inventing new communities and a transparency in our relationships, in government institutions, in society. Very few people question social values. We need to develop an importance on teaching and establishing new value systems in societies and communities, with emphasis on shifting values and practices to unconditional love, kindness and acceptance, rather than status, idealised perfection and elitism, which are all forms of violence on, and repression of, our true human nature.

It is modern society and its corporatized values that are causing most of the malfunctioning. The subtle violence of what society calls normality is disturbing enough and what is expected of people to conform to, in such an environment. That is enough to drive anyone to depression along with the general stress of everyday living and paying ones monthly bills, most people are being denied their humanity. Accepting that our humanity is key in healing, accepting that it is okay to feel broken, deep sadness and the spectrum of emotions that bring us the gifts of questions and answers, help us to get closer to our own inner truth, what is really good for you? What do you really need? How do you really feel? What is really important for the human creature and for the Earth? It is okay to be totally honest and let go, to allow raw emotions to flow through, to just be free to feel what comes through, it's not normal to keep marching on while a war on consciousness is ensuing.

[6] William Manson explains that in 1968, Erich Fromm prophesied "*The year 2000, might be the beginning of a period in which man ceases to be human and becomes transformed into an unthinking and unfeeling machine". -In the context of a prevailing dehuman syndrome, spontaneous human expression becomes pathologised: Being open in speech; being unashamed of one's body; relating to nature; hugging, touching, feeling and making love with other people; refusing to serve in the army and kill; and becoming less dependent on machines are generally considered 'disturbed behaviour' by a society of robopaths". Of course, behavioural modification is facilitated through ideological training, expanding law enforcement, and emotional anaesthesia (psychopharmacology). In my view, revitalisation of one's desiccated human-ness first and foremost requires a renewed contact with the web of evolved life, with Walt Whitman's 'primal sanity of nature'. Transcending the blinkered, bourgeois-utilitarian (mechanistic-industrial) world-view, one can embark on a purification of consciousness, a purging of the detritus of cultural pollution (and a recovery of emotional innocence). Withdrawing from the world of urban commerce (and its mind-numbing "messages"), one severs the flow of media propaganda and ceaseless "information" (relating to the ubiquitous 'buying and selling'). Compulsive 'having' is the pathology of deficient 'being.' Aesthetic simplicity means disconnecting from repulsive superfluity. Seeking sanctuary in wilderness surroundings, one rediscovers the gentler rhythms of low-cost rural living: walking instead of driving, and prevention of disease through a style of living consonant with ecological wisdom.''*-William Manson.

It is definitely a fundamental truth that 'needing and having' are the current basis of what drives Capitalism. Our over-reliance on technology and machines is also driving the unfolding ecocide. This is well illustrated by the story of the Silverback Gorillas in the African Congo. The mining of Gold, Diamonds and Coltan, (geological name - *Columbite Tantalite*), a mineral used in the microchips of every single new electronic device, cell phone or tablet and laptop, comes from the African Congo, Virungas National Park which is a UNESCO World Heritage Site. A biodiverse ecosystem where a small group of the world's last remaining Silverback Gorillas are critically threatened with extinction from poaching and continually reduced habitat due to these existing 'Conflict Minerals' being extracted in the area, that the world is responsible for plundering. Coltan can only be found in a few places in the world, one of which is in Australia, which was the world's largest producer at Wodinga Tantalum mine in Western Australia, however they closed their mine in 2012 because it is cheaper to mine it using slave labour in inhumane conditions in Africa's Democratic Republic of Congo. To make matters worse for the Silverback Gorillas, the SOCO International energy company are pushing to extract gas and oil reserves from under Lake Edward in the National Park, all this, at the cost of one of the last greatest African forests and majestic Gorillas which have only been given an estimated 15 years of survival amidst the adversities they face and through our lack of global responsibility to better manage conservation of such situations, because minerals, gold, diamonds and oil are far more important than saving the Silverback Gorillas and their forest home.

The current psychology behind what drives capitalism cultivates a certain emptiness and spiritual deficit that leads to severe depression and lack of self-worth, when people feel that they have failed society and in societies view have not achieved a desirable status. For some, this leads to severe depression. I have lost several good friends to suicide and there was an element of not feeling useful to society or community that made them feel that way. If we had stronger communities in the West, perhaps such severe depression could be reduced. I understand how it feels to be that despairing. However, I am fortunate enough to be constantly reminded of the love that surrounds me and so I try to pull through, the best I can, even at the worst times, so as to stay here for those who love me and it's not easy to do at times. It is very important to have a supportive community, especially after fifteen years on the path of environmental conservation and seeing that things have become worse for the environment rather than better, due to corporations and politicians arm in arm profiting from environmental destruction. We definitely need to change our psychological and status values in Western society to values that have more depth and meaning for the human spirit. An ecological economy would influence and cultivate healthier values for individuals as well as stronger communities, people could cultivate a self-value that can be attributed to feeling part of a community and caring for the environment, values not based on status, or on consumerist needs and wants that are never deeply fulfilling.

Being as honest with one's self and others as is possible is important, we are not robots, and we are not machines. Being in nature, being creative, painting, writing, singing, and making things; developing projects that could contribute to a better and more harmonious world, playing music or getting involved in a community project or doing something that aids deep relaxation, meditation or trance, all of these things can help bring feelings of deeper fulfilment and bring us more into the moment, reconnecting us with the joy that comes from just being and connecting with others on a deeper level. Reaching out as much as possible to friends and family, without feeling humiliated or the stigma that is carried with the label 'depression' and the negative stigma that go with it such as the words '*mental illness or mental disease*'. Inner work is really important for all of us, not just those of us suffering from depression, but those of us suffering from denial which seems to be the greater problem in human society.

"There is no coming to consciousness without pain. People will do anything, no matter how absurd, in order to avoid facing their own Soul. One does not become enlightened by imagining figures of light, but by making the darkness conscious." ~ Carl Jung

ENDNOTES Chapter 9

1.Dr John Grohol - http://psychcentral.com/lib/what-is-depression-if-not-a-mental-illness/000896

2.Dr Stephan Harding- deep-ecology-hub available online.

3.E.O. Wilson. 'Biophilia' (1984) Published by Harvard University Press

4.Douglas Radmore (2014) Examination of The Biophilia Hypothesis and its implications for Mental Health. Ecopsychology.org

5.David Orr (2004) Love It or Lose It: Earth in Mind. Island Press

6. William Manson (2003) Biophilia: Towards Dehumanisation. Published by theanarchistlibrary.org

Chapter 10: Evolving to Gaia

There are a few speakers on human consciousness and psychology who take into account everything which we experience, even the negative emotions are valuable in indicating our growth and self-nurturing, this is the work of [1]Matt Licata and [2]Jeff Foster. An interesting explanation of depression: Jeff Foster says it is a sign of needing 'Deep Rest', rest from the way you have been living your life, including from thinking we constantly need to achieve, to be perfect, be positive, be this or be that. Being a human being and allowing the space and freedom for emotions to flow without any narrative is a good way to take time out.

Here is something to contemplate: whatever we evolved from, we are all unique expressions of the same form of consciousness that flows through us, we are all perfect as we are, whatever emotional state we experience. The idea that we need to reach a goal to attain a state of constant joy or peace in order to be in harmony with source, is quite dismissive of the infinite nature of creation that we reflect, it is also merciless on our humanity. We were not made to walk around to be blissful forever, human experiences are infinite, infinity is having the ability and freedom to experience the richness of it ***all***, perhaps it is also referred to as 'Free Will' by some...then what we do with our experiences, creates our wisdom, though some of that comes from our soul's knowingness. We have to practice drawing on this inner awareness daily, moment to moment, to let every emotion pass through us, and to see the value of it ***all***, not just that which is enjoyable, good or comfortable, the pain, sadness, loss or grief is just as important in shaping us and directing us to learning about our truer selves and what we do or do not need in our lives to live life on our own terms rather than on the terms of society.

We need reference points, landmarks or the polarities of good and bad to navigate our way through life's experiences, just like we need the illusion of space between objects to be able to judge where to move our bodies in order to get from A to B. If we didn't have these reference points, we wouldn't know what heaven or hell was, but to understand the unity or the grey shades between the polarities, we have to appreciate that we were born with the right to experience it all, therefore, there is no need to become anything other than what we already are, this is what is meant by 'we are already perfect as we are'. We are constantly in the habit of defining ourselves in order to be accepted by society. Perhaps 'unbecoming' or un-defining is part of a daily awareness we could practice, to cure our addiction or need to compartmentalise everything with labels and boxes; or having to reach goal posts and measuring ourselves in terms of what we need to achieve to gain respect from our peers, or to just feel good about ourselves. 'Undefining or unbecoming' is a practice that helps one learn to accept oneself as one is. Letting go of needing to become anything in the process, is the quickest way to step into just 'being', without needing to become anything, such as 'enlightened' or 'perfect'.

"Our world is in crisis because of the absence of consciousness, and so, to whatever degree any one of us can bring back a small piece of the picture and contribute it to the building of the new paradigm, then we participate in the redemption of the human spirit, and that after all is what it's really all about." - Terence McKenna

In addition to my ecology background, I trained as a hypnotherapist, which I was drawn to with an interest in the unconscious mind and emotions. Hypnotherapy has been a tool that I appreciate and respect to access the human subconscious mind and it has also been a gateway to understanding that time is not linear, as humans like to think it is, it could be that parallel realities exist which we can tap into at any point if we desire to. As Quantum physics is beginning to realise that even the smallest particle is affected by our observation of it, this has been scientifically proven, a particle changes its behaviour when we are observing it, the same with trees and plants that have been discovered to communicate on a multi-sensory level, when we become aware of them communicating, they respond to that awareness, again, this is because our consciousness is able to change and morph this reality, because we are part of the multidimensional infinity of divine consciousness. This is not something any external forces could attempt to control, however hard they try.... how can one control consciousness? It simply is not possible.

That intelligent driving force of consciousness wants to be realised in each of us or in each of our souls, this will inevitably happen as we naturally evolve from one level of understanding to another. From the microcosm, we realise that all biological cells work more successfully as a community, performing and functioning more efficiently, the cell biologist [3]Bruce Lipton takes this to a much more profound level in his work, which shows us how we can learn from cell biology to advance human consciousness. More and more scientists are taking courageous steps to unite science and spirituality, risking ridicule, and at times financial sacrifice, because they are seeing how urgent it is for us to enhance our level of consciousness, for ourselves and for the planet.

The evolution of biology, shows us how we naturally progress to the macrocosm from the microcosm, after the realisation that any single cell that becomes self-serving and not functioning for the greater good of the whole, will stop evolving and soon wither and die, as there is nothing else it is in harmony with. This is why we see so much cancer, it is not only a product of pollution and toxicity in our food supply but it is a product of the self-serving values and a lack of understanding how connected to our environment we are. These unhealthy values which exist in human beliefs, are increasing human disease such as cancer and other illnesses. These are biological manifestations of the malfunctioning deformations, which we have created as a product of our thinking that we are separate from our environment, the universe and beyond, (the macrocosm).

We could say that sustainable biological cells are those that are constantly working as communities, evolving to become higher more advanced life forms and that these life forms have achieved harmony through co-creation which has helped species evolve through 3.5 billion years on the planet. We can see this from the beginning of life on Earth with the early single cells evolving to our current biodiversity of elaborations of cell communities, forming complex and more advanced creatures from insects to large mammals and plants such as trees and Earth itself as a Gaia formation of trillions of co-creating living systems of elaborate biological communities. All in harmony with one another, everything that exists, apart from us, realises naturally, that it is part of an infinite god consciousness, just by the expression of being and living and even dying. While today, despite our human intelligence, we see some humans are more like self-serving cells that malfunction that become dysfunctional, destructive and cancerous when we see ourselves as superior to or separate from nature, whereas those of us that feel connected to nature are the more harmonious, self-sustaining ones and possibly we have a chance of evolving to higher states of consciousness.

We humans are a bit slow, despite what we think is our superior intelligence to other creatures, because we have allowed ourselves to become conditioned by certain misconceptions such as the idea that we are separate from Nature, consciousness, or the 'God' label. The ultimate change from this paradigm to a more harmonious one, may, or may not happen in our lifetime, but it is an inevitability which is unstoppable; and despite the severe environmental destruction that is driven by human financial greed, the survival of the 'fittest' humans now depends on our level of consciousness and if we have the ability to make the leap to develop the necessary parts of our spiritual awareness, that reconnects us with nature and the Earth. This is the ecology of consciousness and evolution on a spiritual level. It is part of our mission to evolve to higher states of consciousness, which is the macrocosmic seed. Consciousness (God) is Love and wants us to realise that we are part of this infinite co-creation.

Perhaps we needed to create a 'them' and 'us' illusion to facilitate this realisation. Hopefully no longer at the price of the planet and our fellow creatures misery and suffering, or extinction. I have, until now, thought that will be the outcome, as we are living in an anthropogenically driven environmental crisis. However, I now have a renewed hope and faith as I have had my own personal inner understanding of what I attempt to explain in words here, words detract from the experience of infinite Love, that is a potential seed laying in all of us waiting for each of us to awaken to our ability and power to co-create with the creator, a new and more harmonious way of being aligned with Gaia, the Earth and the Cosmos.

Human well-being & Earth well-being are inseparable and have become increasingly important to many of us. It is our right to be able to protect both these aspects of ecological well-being, which is rapidly being ignored by the predatory aspect of Capitalism and human greed. We are our environment, therefore healing ourselves and creating inner-peace, creates outer peace for the planet, this concept has arisen out of our realisation, which we need to re-create cohesion between 'Human well-being & Earth well-being'. Basically, this states that human ecology is intrinsically connected to the Earth's Ecology. This is the ecology of reclaiming our connection, not only with Earth but with the cosmos and universal consciousness.

[4]Jose Arguilles said *" it is not Earth that needs saving, it's humanity that needs to save itself from itself."*

There are growing numbers of people all over the planet who are now seeking inner equilibrium due to a growing awakening to the fact that we are all connected, and not separate from our environment. Ecological devastation and human devastation are two sides of the same global disease, which can only be correctly understood and overcome by understanding we are part of the whole ecology of living, that has not been functioning harmoniously. If we are to survive with the planet, we must now seek inner equilibrium.

"Repression of the ecological unconscious is the deepest root of many of the psychological, social, ecological, spiritual, and physical problems in contemporary industrial society. Ecocidal policies do not only attack and devastate 'external' nature but our 'internal' natures as well. This is why deep ecology is about 'Restoring the Earth, Healing the Mind" - [5]Theodore Roszak

Indigenous people have always had a natural understanding of our connection to the Earth and a deep respect for Nature. However, we have distanced ourselves from Nature through the rise and development of technology and industry in western civilization. Eco-psychology is an important aspect of deep ecology, which was originally founded much earlier, some say in the 1970s with the work of [6]Arne Naess. It is the closest we have in western civilization to understanding the importance of our connection with nature. Though the concepts of environmental conservation and importance of ecology can be seen to have emerged from earlier, as in the 1800s, when John Muir, the American naturalist, writer and conservationist, founded the Sierra Club and Yosemite National Park. He saw even then, the encroaching dangers of industrialisation on the natural environment. The sixties were an important contribution to the evolving of this understanding, because the development of peace and social justice gave strength to the environmental movement and the work of people like [7]Rachel Carson. Her book '*The Silent Spring*' which was published in 1962, is a key book that gave rise to principles in deep ecology. It was one of the first books to educate the public on the concepts of ecosystems and how they connect us to our environment in terms of human health and environmental health, those being one and the same thing. It was one of the most profound books on my university reading list and perhaps that is why it has partly inspired the title of this book. Whatever toxins we release into the environment affect species, ecosystems and eventually come back to us as health problems. When we pollute the environment, what we do to the environment, in turn affects us inevitably, as we are our environment, yet the majority of people wish to ignore this important reality.

Deep ecological principles have had some strong criticism in the past, including that of being a movement which hates humanity. That is just one opinion. A fresh perspective is needed. Quantum science is a fast developing field connected to deep ecology, in the sense that humans are still evolving mentally and on a consciousness level rather than biologically. It is even possible that our cell biology can still change or be affected by a shift in consciousness. Even today, there are countless cases of people that have cured themselves of fatal illnesses, disease or cancerous tumours by working through previous misconceptions about themselves and were able to heal and cure themselves, are they tapping into the quantum field for healing? We have not stopped evolving, what we are doing to our environment, we are doing to ourselves, we need to respond to this with a shift in our human understanding that the environmental crisis is an indication that human consciousness has to change. We could see this present time as a wake-up call and a chance to make changes internally and externally, in terms of learning from our mistakes, rather than being hateful to humanity. It is a true and popular analogy among environmentalists that we are like a cancer on earth at the moment; though with all illness and diseases, it is usually an indication that we need to re-evaluate how we live our lives on this planet. So just like when we get sick we need to change how we nourish ourselves internally, mentally, spiritually, emotionally and physically, we must do the same and change the way in which we live with the Earth. We can seize this time as an opportunity to review our relationship with what we previously saw as a separate environment, and nurture a better understanding, respect and love of ourselves in terms of birthing a new a perspective on ecology at a spiritual level.

As discussed in the previous chapter, many of us feel anger and grief with the environmental destruction that human greed is causing; we can use that anger and grief in a constructive way, to motivate us to create change and take action. By embracing a more sustainable and ecological lifestyle, we create self-empowerment, confidence, nurturing inner nourishment and inner peace.

[8] The scientist James Lovelock used to work for NASA and during the 1960s, he started working on the Gaia Hypothesis, this showed scientifically and ecologically that Earth is an organism made up of ecological units that act synchronistically to create this Planet-sized super-organism. Human consciousness is an ecological issue because we need to evolve human consciousness to understand that all life on Earth has *a consciousness*, an energy that flows through all biological forms, that is just as powerful as our own and we all share this connection, it doesn't matter how complex or simple the life forms appear, they all share the same energy that flows through them, which I refer to as *consciousness.*

[9] Dr. Ashok Khosla, president of the IUCN (International Union for the Conservation of Nature) has taken this study a step further to bring people's attention to show that all life forms have some level of consciousness and how deeply intrinsically human consciousness affects all life on this planet. He gave a demonstration to show this with an electromagnetic experiment on plants.

How does the electro-magnetic plant device work? Based upon a device originally developed by Volney Mathison back in the 1940's, it works by using a Wheatstone bridge, which is an ultra-sensitive circuit that can detect the slightest change of electrical resistance in the plants and translate them through sounds or lights also connected to the circuit. These electrical signals may be one millionth of a volt. All living organisms, whether mammals, amphibians, or plants, have subtle electrical signals running through them. In humans, the brain communicates through the nervous system to control organs, our brains, limbs and sight, using weak electrical charges. As recounted by [10] Peter Tompkins and Christopher Bird in their 1973 book "The Secret Life of Plants", several different scientists had conducted such experiments. You connect two receivers of the circuit, one to the root of the plant and the second to a leaf. They then connect the meter to a trigger, a voltage-controlled synthesiser or similar device. The change in the plant's electrical resistance controls the pitch, volume and filtering if the measurements are translated through sound synthesis, as the plant responds to what it is sensing in its external environment and what is happening around it.

Research has found that plants react to their surroundings and they also communicate with one another. Light, water, sound, and even emotional energy within a room that a plant is placed in, all cause significant alterations to the plant's electrical current. As Dr Ashok Khosla, explains that each plant also has its own unique sound signature, or its own 'song'. Now that people are beginning to understand how plants read and respond to their environment, we begin to understand that plants have a kind of consciousness as they even react to what we are going to do before we do it, or to our emotions, many experiments have shown this.

[11] Norman Lederman was the true pioneer of reading plants that way and he put on the world's first live plant concert in quadraphonic sound, at the Kreeger Music Building's, McDonald Recital Hall back on April 17th, 1974.

[12] Suzanne Simard, forest ecologist at the University of British Columbia has been studying old trees in forest ecosystems and how they communicate with other trees through root systems. These 'Grandmother' trees transport nutrients through root systems, to younger trees when they need it. How does an older tree know when

a younger tree needs these nutrients? It is a complex system of chemical communication through their roots and a giant network of fungi, some of which are mycorrhizal fungi that have a symbiotic relationship with these trees. The whole of the forest is connected by this network of fungal threads and Simard's research reveals that when a Grandmother Tree is cut down, the survival rate of the younger members of the forest is diminished.

This interactive communicating community of trees, are not just using chemical signals, but also an awareness of consciousness, of sensing in their way, what is going on in their external environment, an environment to which they are deeply connected both biologically and on sensory levels which we are still trying to understand. This is even more reason why it is important to preserve ancient trees in forest ecosystems.

There is some pioneering research being done with plant consciousness which will eventually help us advance our own level and understanding of the field of consciousness and our connectivity to all living beings, especially if we begin to realise that despite plants being seen as lower life forms, they respond to our thoughts and feelings as they respond to other plants and animals around them. If plants display this level of consciousness, we have not only greatly misunderstood plants, but have even more so deeply misunderstood animal intelligence, sentience and consciousness and our cruel exploitation and abuse of animals is even more unjustifiable.

[13]The Heart Math Institute has shown how the human heart and brain act as radio transmitters and receivers affecting and being affected by other energy fields. We emit a large toroidal energy field generated from our hearts beating and we are affected by Electromagnetic Energy of the synthetic and organic kind, everything is made up of electromagnetic energy and everything generates an electromagnetic pulse and field. We are even affected by synthetic electromagnetic energy, given out by mobile phone towers and satellite systems, it has been shown in recent scientific studies that the cells of plants and trees are negatively affected by signals from mobile phones and phone towers. The electromagnetic

waves of present communication and man-made sonar systems are affecting wildlife in many detrimental ways, including the navigational abilities of whales, dolphins, birds and bees which could explain why they have been dying in significant numbers due to this form of electromagnetic vibrational and noise pollution.

When we look at how everything that is alive also has an intelligent consciousness flowing through it, this reminds us of quantum physics again, because we are seeing that when we observe a particle, it behaves differently, that means that either the particle itself is displaying some form of consciousness, being conscious that we are observing it or our very observation of it changes its behaviour. Ancient indigenous concepts teach us that we can begin to heal the more fundamental alienation, between our lost connection with the natural environment and our ancient tribal knowledge. We as humans can re-establish this relationship with Nature and the cosmos as one being and not separate entities. That is a true form of ecological spiritual rebirth that indigenous peoples understand as cosmo-vision.

Deep Ecology is a blend of certain ancient indigenous concepts with modern concepts. We are part of the Earth's consciousness and she is part of the sacred feminine and masculine, the deeper fabric of our consciousness in the web all life that flows through all beings. The corporatisation of the political world has become unethical and careless, ignoring its responsibility to protect the planet. Unconsciously, some of us take on this violence imposed on the Earth, internalising it. Those of us who are aware of this, are carrying the burden of responsibility, grief, guilt and loss, especially when we see ecocide unfolding on a daily basis with destruction of key ecosystems such as our forests and oceans. At the other extreme, some of us have become so de-sensitised to this that the easiest option is denial. We need to find ways to understand why we are feeling powerless to affect the overwhelming crisis in which we are living.

We each have a responsibility to expand our understanding of ourselves in relation to nature in the modern world, but with reacceptance of the ancient indigenous beliefs, that all life is sacred and intrinsically affected by our actions, and even our thoughts. Only then will we evolve and start living more ecologically on the Earth. Implementing sustainability and human sovereignty is a human right and need, as well as a necessary way for Earth's resources to be managed within Nature's natural carrying capacity.

Many experts around the world are working towards reclaiming lost and ancient indigenous knowledge. Through transformation power of these concepts and how reclaiming the spiritual ecology with our connection with Gaia, Pacha Mama, Madre Tierra, Mother Earth and Cosmos are a step towards creating and mapping a new more harmonious world and reality. Some ways in which to connect with Nature on a deeper level, are to work with the plant teachers through ancient medicinal entheogens with a highly experienced Indigenous Shaman. Other ways to reconnect with Nature is simply being in Nature as much as one possibly can.

ENDNOTES: Chapter 10

1. Psychologist Matt Licata –A loving Healing Space- alovinghealingspace.blogspot.in

2. Jeff Foster, Author, Teacher- lifewithoutacentre.com

3. Bruce Lipton (Nov 30, 2007) *Biology of Belief*. Pulisher- Mountain of Love; First Edition

4. Jose Arguilles (September 6, 2011) *Manifesto for the Noosphere: The Next Stage in the Evolution of Human Consciousness.* Evolver Editions.

5. Theodore Roszack (1995) *Ecopsychology. Restoring the Earth Restoring the Mind.* Sierra Club books.

6. Arne Naess (1998) *Ecology, Community and Lifestyle: Outline of an Ecosophy.* Cambridge University Press.

7. Rachel Carson (1962) *Silent Spring.* First Marina Books.

8. James Lovelock (2010) *Gaia, A New Look At Life On Earth*. Oxford University Press.

9. Dr Ashok Khosla. IUCN President- http://iucn.org/news_homepage/?8804/IUCN-President-gets-top-WWF-honours

10. Peter Tompkins and Christopher Bird (1st December 1973) *The Secret Life of Plants*. Harper and Row.

11. Norman Lederman. *Herb 'n' Electrics:* Stereofernic Orchistra

12. Suzanne W. Simard, David A. Perry2, Melanie D. Jones, David D. Myrold, Daniel M. Durall and Randy Molina. .*Net transfer of carbon between ectomycorrhizal tree species in the field.* (16 May 1997) Nature 388, 579-582

13. Institute of HeartMath - www.heartmath.org

Chapter 11: The Birth of Solutions

There is a very clear suppression of many important areas of science, ancient knowledge and ancient technologies. Since the birth of civilisations, governments have been burning libraries and destroying knowledge that threatens their power. We are currently seeing the result of the destruction and suppression of this knowledge and science at the cost of Earth's natural resources and human life. There are many technologies, modern and lost that have been purposely suppressed, these unpublicised sacrifices have put us in the position in which we are today. We did not just arrive here through ignorance. Humanity is being kept in a purposeful suspension that will only lead to our own demise. It is beyond the capacity of any investigator or researcher to recover completely, or rediscover, all of the knowledge which has been suppressed or lost. While that is not the goal of this book, we do need to consider a few examples of what is being suppressed in order to give the reader a different perspective on things, and so I have revealed a few examples in earlier chapters. We do need to acknowledge that we are not given access to full scientific knowledge in modern society, some of it is missing from public education for various reasons, mainly to keep power where it is at present.

"American and British history is riddled with examples of valid research and inventions which have been suppressed and spoken against by the conventional science community. This has been of great cost to society and to individual scientists. Rather than furthering the pursuit of new scientific frontiers, the structure of British and American scientific institutions leads to conformity and furthers consensus-seeking. Scientists are generally like other people when it comes to the biases and self-justifications that cause them to make bad decisions and evade the truth. Some topics in science are 'taboo' subjects. Two examples are the field of psychic phenomenon and the field of new energy devices such as cold fusion. Journals, books and internet sites exist for those scientists who want an alternative to the present conformist scientific venues." – [1] J. Sacherman

A very important aspect of ecological science is how all biological life generates electrical impulses. The Earth also pulses and has unseen energy lines (ley lines), made up of electrical currents that provide a global electrical circuit much like the human energy meridians, upon which the 8000-year-old Chinese medicine is founded.

[2]Hugh Newman has been doing some interesting research on these natural energy lines in the Earth at ancient Palaeolithic sites around the globe, to learn how the ancients developed technologies using granite stone structures to tap into this energy and so increase the fertility of plant seedlings and increase crop yields. He has developed some interesting theories and ideas that connect to human and Earth consciousness through studying the ancients and their use of granite stone structures.

[3]George Van Tassel's work also involved a large granite stone, believed by ancient native indigenous to be a sacred stone, it was a giant bolder simply named "Giant Rock" presumed to be the world's largest free-standing boulder at the time. There is a carved sign of a scorpion on the northern side of the rock, a sign which was only carved by Native Americans for very special sites. This site was used for special ceremonies by chief shamans to get in touch with inter-dimensional spirits, to talk to the spirit men of the rock, the ceremony would go on for three days. The spirits of the rock or the rock people prophesized that one day the rock would split in two, symbolising the beginning of a new era. The rock did indeed split in two following a group meditation by a modern day Asian shaman in Feb, 2000. However, before that happened, George Van Tassel had built an airfield on the site and he became interested in the special energy of the site, he began to meditate frequently at giant rock until one time he claimed he made contact with an alien being that he believed used the rock as a portal. This being shared some knowledge with George which led him to build the Integratron, a time machine for basic research on cell rejuvenation, anti-gravity and time travel. The domed building is 55 feet in diameter and consisted of four floors. Its essential core design was that it was built over a magnetic vortex and its materials were non-metallic. It's

functioning was built on the principles and understanding of the Earth's magnetic field.

Giant Rock was believed to have the same Harmonic value as the Pyramid of Giza, There is definitely something very special about the properties of granite, as many ancient sacred sites are made from granite stones including ancient Fougos (granite stone structures that one can enter into a cavernous hole), which were used as places to use dreams as a means to connect with the spirit world. Having slept in a Fougo myself as a volunteer for someone else's research, I definitely felt that my dreams were affected or amplified in some way. Many of these ancient stones are strategically placed over the Earth's ley lines or energy meridians and some of these sacred stone granite sites are believed to be portals to multi-dimensional realms such as Aramu Maru, the door carved into a giant granite rock in Hayu Marca mountain, Peru. Indigenous local people have countless stories of people disappearing into other worlds through that doorway.

What did the ancient people of the megalithic civilisations and other lost civilisations know with how to use granite as a key between enhancing Earth energies to cosmic energies? There seem to be many indications in ancient technologies towards this lost knowledge. George Van Tassel was definitely on to something with his research and device to tap into those energies, but he died of a heart attack before completing his building of the Integratron, it is very similar to the work of [4]Wilhelm Reich, who studied and experimented with the same energy field which he called Orgone, but that the Chinese call Chi energy and the Yogis call Kundalini energy.

Further studies by [5]Dr Masuru Emoto, show how human thoughts and emotions have a dramatic effect on water crystals. Dr Emoto took photographs using a high definition microscope of water whilst it was being exposed to intense human emotions, he has also performed similar scientific experiences with rice and demonstrated clearly how human thought affects the decomposition of rice and other organic substances over a period of time. These experiments have become so popular, that there are endless videos on the internet of homemade filmed experiments of the famous Emoto rice trials, where cooked rice is put into three separate containers, one is ignored, the other exposed to negative emotions and one exposed to positive emotions, there is definitely a consensus according to the general public that Dr Emoto's experiments work and the rice exposed to positive emotions lasts the longest. As we are made up of 65 percent water, you can become conscious of how your thoughts affect biological systems including your own body water stored in your cells and how this amplifies your internal emotional ecology and affects your body and well-being. This in itself, shows us how we must take more responsibility for our thoughts and emotions.

Native American Medicine Wheel Healing also shows that human consciousness with intent, can heal the Earth and even affect Earth changes. [6]Blue Thunder, (Bennie LeBeu) is a Native American Medicine Wheel Healer whom I had the privilege of meeting in Guatemala, where he was invited to do some healing as Guatemala has a tragic history of indigenous genocide some 40 years ago. His work is well known and demonstrates how powerful human intent is, if used in a healing ritual process with the Earth energies, around some of the most powerful meridian energy ley lines on Earth.

We are living in a time when we are at war with everything in order to preserve our health, our environment, our minds, our human rights, our hearts, our fellow creatures, and even fighting for the right to choose how we farm and what we eat. This is literally a war on human survival and human consciousness; a war pushed upon us by the oligarchy, a war that we were blindly coerced and trapped into, and in ways we are unwilling supporters as we are a part of this system.

We have all the technology, knowledge and means, for healthy living, local organic food production, alternative health medicine and the array of alternative cancer cures from hemp oil, to rainforest plant medicines, coconut oil, sodium bicarbonate and black salve. These are just some of the few natural cures for cancer that would disable the multi-million pharmaceutical industry. Indigenous cultures have developed their own deep understanding of plant medicine. Working with the Shiwiar people in the Amazon rainforest gave me a glimpse into the incredible wealth of knowledge which they carry in their memories, on each plant in the rainforest and its medicinal benefits. A wealth of knowledge is fast disappearing with the destruction of the rainforests.

If we replaced food scarcity with sustainable food security by growing it and managing food resources locally, we would disable the bio-engineering industries, there simply would be no need for them in that respect. There is a resistance in the government and the oil industry inhibiting cleaner energy and more environmentally friendly technologies for cars. There have been a long list of solar, compressed air and water-fuel cars that have failed to go on the public market either due to patent dismissal, government dismissal or lack of funding, such as the Japanese company's water car that Genopax tried to launch in 2011, but they lacked the finances and governments will not subsidise such projects because an invention of a water-fuel car that could use seawater or any other kind of water, would completely destabilise the oil economy and the huge profit governments make from the oil industry. Then, as you learned in earlier chapters of this book, we have a variety of functioning Free Energy devices in operation using different methods as demonstrated by Sir John Searl and Patrick Kelly, which could revolutionise transport in many ways and be used to power domestic and industrial scale set-ups efficiently without any impact on the environment. These technologies would put vehicles and home electricity on a parallel with our Internet wireless technologies. We could live in a world where we would never see drought or people without clean and abundant fresh water.

Patrick Kelly has details on his websites to build devices that suck water out of the air, and then there is Trevor James Constable's technology that cleaned air pollution and could put an end to deserts and famine, if we understand more about the aether. However, aether science is not regarded by mainstream science as a serious science, yet it must be taken more seriously. All these technologies exist and could be implemented; the only problem is we cannot expect them to be implemented with the current corrupt power system that functions only for financial profit and not for the good of mankind or for environmental conservation. I hope that the information provided in this book will help people become more self-reliant and inspire some folk to create their own local, cleaner energy technologies. The photovoltaic solar industry is also advancing to new realms and we can look forward to using new technologies such as the new pioneering advanced battery systems that companies like Tesla have created that can store the energy from the Sun or wind power. The present problem is that these systems are still too expensive for everyone to afford. Prices will go down though as these technologies become more available on demand. The technologies that meet the greatest resistance are those directly threatening the fossil-fuel industries. Perhaps if more sentient and aware people in positions of power learned about the truth they would support the cause for change but for now we have to take responsibility to make the change in as many ways as we can in our local and global communities.

Many people are feeling overwhelmed by current world events. Some feel that the global level of political corruption is so deep that there is nothing we can do to change things. These people will often use the words 'us' and 'them', with 'them' being the oligarchy, the elite, the control system, or as many know them, their secret societies such as the Illuminati. It is easy to feel overwhelmed when you become aware of these issues, however, people keep affirming a victim mentality with believing that 'the governments have ultimate control'. It is only our conditioned victim-mentality that gives 'them' such powers. It is definitely a daily discipline to decondition oneself from the victim frame of thinking which is reinforced through the mainstream media, it is a deep conditioning in which we all have been playing a part.

The current 'control system' is only operating from one tiny low vibrational field of consciousness, which is limited by our belief that 'they' are all powerful, however, 'they' are only motivated by their fear of us realising the truth and their arrogance that they are more powerful than the natural course of spiritual and ecological evolution of consciousness, which is taking place now, it will take each of us to realise that we are co-creating the reality which we are experiencing.

This control system wants us to feel diminished and helpless, yet it cannot control a human being who realises that s/he is no longer a victim in the new reality of awakening. Whilst we discover that we are unlimited multi-sensory beings who can shape our own reality, because we are part of a multi-dimensional universe which is infinite and ever changing. The environmental crisis is a crisis of human understanding, although human consciousness is changing in the face of destruction, in the same way that one can find a diamond under the thousands of years of pressures that created coal, the rapid destruction and increasing greed can actually function as a driving force to awaken us much faster.

We are forming a global tribe of caring, conscious and active beings, doing many important things. We must focus on the solutions to move into a new paradigm of conscious living, aligned with planetary and universal harmony. Our global tribes are now gathering momentum in the millions, this is an indication things are changing. It is a crucial time to take your attention away from what the corrupt system is doing, and focus with intention, using your mind and your heart, on what you want to see the world change into, for the benefit of both Earth and your children. By doing this, we can terraform the future survival of humanity with intention, so imagine the world in which you want to live. This in itself is powerful. If enough of us are using our intention and we meditate on opening doors to manifest a new reality on many levels, then that will happen. We can create practical sustainable communities, or by using the internet locate suitable existing communities, or we can work together to create them. There are some great resources out there, you don't necessarily need to have money to own land to do this, there are many ways you can be a part of a community without needing to use your own savings. We have to embrace every opportunity we can to be sustainable whether we are in a city or urban community or in the country. You can move somewhere where you can easily access the land and work with other communities to grow food. If you live in a city, find ways to support organic and sustainable communities or community farms in your area, and get involved in some active way. From my own sources, I know of incredible things happening, where more and more people are using alternative energy devices at different locations around the world for the benefit of their communities.

Humans are extremely resilient. The Earth is resilient too, and she is very strong. This is a time that requires practical action from humans because governments and corporations are not going to change their motives or behaviour, so we have to become the ambassadors for the Earth and each take responsibility and transform our lives to become self-reliant. We must put our intent where there are solutions, and take our focus away from the darkness. The light needs to gather momentum now, so that we can make the change quickly in order to build bridges to a new paradigm.

Be discerning, we do need to be aware that there are some false movements out there, as well as false gurus and teachers. I worked for a time as an ecological consultant for one such popular movement, popular in the eyes of the so called awake and aware communities. We then discovered that they planned to develop large cities in the pristine rainforests of Latin America, without consideration to preserving these highly endangered ecosystems. Wouldn't it be better for a foundation that claims itself to be 'conscious' and 'sustainable', instead to purchase vast areas of wasteland to develop these sustainable and ecological cities? Wouldn't that be a more inspirational and desirable goal to build conscious cities or communities on reclaimed wasteland instead? When you do support or join a website that represents such movements, it is more powerful and practical to look locally or join an actual sustainable community rather than a website that claims to provide the solutions for humanity, but shows no signs of doing the actual practical logistical aspect.

Becoming self-sufficient internally, with ourselves first, instead of following others whom we hope have all the answers, takes strength. This points towards ourselves becoming emotionally mature and nurturing an internal awareness. If we don't understand the lessons which life throws at us, then we will continue to make the same mistakes and be unable to break old patterns. The only way forward in self-development is to do the inner work. Outwardly, we will start to experience and become richer with our experiences in communicating with others and daily exchanges. We are so addicted to seeking answers from others and following others, it is as addictive as heroine and could ultimately lead to lack of inner nurturing as well as leading lots of people to another dead end. The energetic ecology of the internal body is profoundly connected to the energetic ecology of the Earth and the universe.

Nothing stays the same, everything changes. In realising that we are multi-sensory beings and that this reality is a fictional construction dictated to us, we are no longer victims of it. I hear people talk about the oligarchy as 'them verses us'. There is no 'them' at the end of this realisation, there is only 'us' and no matter how cheesy it sounds, we are the solution. If we are able to realise this and many of us are able to, then their attempt to control us are failing miserably.

This is not something any elite 1 percent can attempt to control, however hard they try.... how can one control God consciousness? It is simply not possible. This is where the elite show themselves to be ignorant or blinded by their short-sighted addiction to power and limited by being trapped in the low vibrational field which they have built for themselves – a field that cannot be sustained in an infinitely changing universe, change that we can create and which affects us all.

Consciousness, or the intelligent self-aware energy that flows through all living things including Earth, is the embodiment of love, this love wants to be realised in each of us or at least somewhere deep inside each of our souls, this will inevitably happen, as we naturally evolve from one level of consciousness to another, this natural rule applies to humans.

We can see this from the beginning of life on Earth, almost 3.5 billion years ago, with the early single cells evolving to our current level of enriched biodiversity, single cells have evolved to the most sophisticated complex communities from insects to large mammals and plants such as trees and Earth itself as a super organism. All functioning in harmony with one another, everything that exists apart from us, works in perfect harmony, now it's our turn to do the same.

We humans are a bit slower because we have allowed ourselves to become conditioned by certain misconceptions such as the idea that we are separate from God consciousness or infinity. Some of us are getting there at our own rate although painfully...The ultimate change from this paradigm to a more harmonious one may not happen in our lifetime but it is an inevitable and unstoppable. It is part of our mission to evolve to higher states of consciousness, which is the microcosmic seed. The basis of all religions and spirituality is the principle that '*God is Love*' and this higher form of consciousness wants us to realise that we are part of this infinite co-creation, though we go around fighting over whose 'God' is more superior and are still very much at a low plateau of consciousness.

We have the opportunity to lay the foundations for a new world. This is the hidden message in this Silent Ecocide which is constantly reiterated in indigenous prophesies of end times. *The Last Voices of Gaia* is a phrase that came to me some years ago, as a way to describe those of us that are currently speaking out for the protection of planet Earth. We are indigenous peoples and westerners, arm in arm, forming an ever-growing global community of conscious people, visionaries, scientists, whistleblowers, ex-military, environmentalists, artists, inventors and solution energy engineers, around the world who have a vision of humanity and Earth having a different future. We are aware that we are not being given the full truth about our past, let alone our present. What unites us all is our concern for the survival of the planet, while we witness the rapid destruction of the natural environment by governments and corporate giants.

Gaia is a Greek word for 'Earth' and the name has later been adapted by people such as James Lovelock to the 'Gaia hypothesis' to describe Earth as a planet made up of different ecosystems that create a macro super organism that is a living breathing conscious Earth being. Many feel that Gaia embodies Earth as being consciousness. There are ancient indigenous legends over the globe from the Hopi Indians and Mayan legends, to the Australian Aboriginals, each story suggests that humans must unite with Gaia, Pacha Mama or Madra Tierra consciousness, also referred to as Cosmovision by the elders, where human consciousness is deeply connected with the Earth and the Cosmos. The energetic ecology of the internal body is profoundly connected to the energetic ecology of the Earth and universe.

[7]Tribal leaders of the Hopi prophesied that during the end times, the Earth would be crossed by iron snakes (oil pipelines) and stone rivers (roads) and the land would be chequered by giant cobwebs (geo-engineering), spun back and forth in the sky and seas will turn black (oil pollution or de-oxygenation).

Though some may say that the Mayans are responsible for everyone thinking that the world would end in a devastating apocalypse in 2012 simply because the calendar did not continue onwards, they never made any such prediction. It was Hollywood's and even the alternative media's interpretation that promoted this idea, they were a civilisation that existed until 1000 AD, remains of their fascinating cities can be found in their pyramid ruins such as at Palenque in the rainforests of Central America. They were famous for keeping exquisitely detailed calendars carved in stone which indicated that they were excellent astronomers. They predicted that mankind would collapse after earthquakes, volcanoes and floods. The Mayan god Kulkulan was the equivalent to the Aztec priest king Quetzalcoatl, often depicted as a feathered serpent deity, who represents forces of good and light, the legend says he would appear on Earth to restore natural harmony to Earth and humanity.

The Australian Aboriginals believe that earthquakes and tidal waves will come as a sign of end times. Guboo Ted Thomas, a Yuin Nation Elder told of earthquakes and tidal waves will happen in our final days as a reminder because we don't consider Earth as our mother, then a powerful wave, not a tidal wave but a spiritual wave, will come and show people they need to love one another and we need to stop seeing ourselves as separate from nature, '*We have taken away the balance and we are not putting it back*'.- Guboo Ted Thomas

There are countless other indigenous prophesies that describe a time where man is at end times, but they also say that some form of transition in consciousness has to take place for life on Earth to continue. It is very clear that this is the reality in which we currently find ourselves. If we are to continue surviving on this planet, Then we need to change the way in which we manage natural resources, we need to change the foundations of economy, we must put value on unseen goods and services that nature provides us and decentralise management of resources to local management, or return to each country its right to self-manage its own natural resources and minerals and water, food and energy resources. If we want to take good care of the environment, then local management of natural resources is the most environmentally friendly way to do so.

Perhaps we needed to create a 'them' and 'us' illusion to facilitate this realisation. I hope it is no longer at the price of the planet or the misery, suffering or extinction of our fellow creatures. I have up till now thought that the outcome for Earth will be a bleak one, as we are living in the most destructive and violent time of human history. However, I do have a renewed seedling of hope, a potential seed laying in all of us, waiting for each individual to awaken to our ability and power to co-create with the creator a new and more harmonious reality aligned with the ecology of the Planet.

Destruction, exploitation and conflict are driven by human insecurity, unrest and greed which can only be resolved by creating inner peace. The environmental crisis is a crisis of human consciousness. We have lost our true sense of humanity, our ancient spiritual connection with the Earth and cosmos has been violated and forgotten, the sacred masculine and feminine have been exploited, humiliated and perverted, our communities fragmented through fear, our governments are blinded by the love of money and power instead of serving the best interests of humanity or preserving the Earth.

It was Jimi Hendrix who said quite simply '*When the love of power is overcome by the power of love, only then will the world know Peace*'. This is why we must transform and heal our deepest inner being, saving the world and humanity is now an inside job. Anything you or I do externally to take action cannot be sustained until humanity has also taken action to do inner work to nurture inner peace, this will then be reflected outwardly and we will see a new way of being unfold. Abundance, harmony and peace could be the future for humanity and the environment. Every living creature that is a part of the Earth will resonate with the internal understanding that we are all connected to the Earth, Cosmos and one another. Only then will humans treat each other with the respect and gratitude that reflects this understanding.

The world is beginning to acknowledge that indigenous people are the best conservationists, from the Masai in Africa, to the Indians who lived with tigers, over to the indigenous people of the Amazon rainforest, seeing as they are the only global people who have continually lived in harmony with the land, what affects the land affects them. They have a natural understanding of deep ecological principles, they have no interest in money nor do they need to be a part of the western world, as they are completely self-sufficient, whereas our 'civilized' society has created vulnerable dependant humans who have forgotten the basics of how to survive in Nature, let alone how to respect Nature, therefore instead we are serving dysfunctional governments rather than taking care of the Earth.

It is the tradition of the Shiwiar to sow their guests with sharing a fermented brew called Chicha. Photo credit. Samuel Remerand, August 2012.

By comparison, as indigenous people have no vested interest in our world, they continue to be genuinely motivated without financial agendas, purely to defend Nature and their ancestral lands from corporate and governmental exploitation. Indigenous people have been warning white men for years of the destruction and mistakes that will be made. Indigenous people are exemplary custodians of the Planet and they deserve the highest respect and should be given the highest authority by governing systems over serious conservation policies, treaties, conventions and agreements.

ENDNOTES: Chapter 11

1. J.Sacherman (1997) *Cognitive Processes and the Suppression of Sound Scientific Ideas*. On line internet available

2. Hugh Newman (2010) *Earth Grids*, the Secret Pattern of Gaia's Sacred Sites.

3. George Van Tassel (1957) *The Council of Seven Lights*. Devores and Co. Publishers.

4. Wilhem Reich (1973) *Ether, God & Devil & Cosmic Superimposition*. Farrar, Straus and Giroux; First Edition
5. Dr Masuru Emoto (September 20, 2005) *The Hidden Messages in Water*. Atria Books.
6. Bennie E. LeBeau Sr. (2014) *Healing Mother Earth's Sacred Sites with the Medicine Wheel – How Life Force Energy Works*. Earth Wisdom Foundation.

7. Will Anderson. (2001) *Earth Mother Crying. Prophesy Seekers Trilogy*

Chapter 12: Walk with Nature

"There is something in the human spirit that will survive and prevail, there is a tiny and brilliant light burning in the heart of man that will not go out no matter how dark the world becomes." -Leo Tolstoy.

The solutions, technologies, concepts and initiatives presented in this book are already being implemented and those who are implementing them are the bridge builders from an old, out-dated paradigm to a new way of being with one another and with planet Earth. This book presents so many alternative technologies and concepts and connects those of us that are making lifestyle changes to have less of a human imprint on the environment or other species, we are the seeds of change. Hope is with those of us who are pioneers of crypto-currencies, open-source software and alternative energy pioneers and designers of alternative natural capital and green economic systems. Hope is with those of us who have built or are forming alternative conscious communities. Hope is with those of us who are relocating to places where we can have more control over these choices and create new societies, until the waves of the collective consciousness are strong enough to make the leap of faith to a more holistic, unified humanity, living harmoniously with Planet Earth. Hope is kept alive through individuals and communities willing to take action internally and externally for the good of the Earth. We cannot sit back and wait for someone else to take responsibility or we will be complicit in this silent ecocide.

A gradual development of strong community systems locally and worldwide for sustainable living methods, will give us an expanding autonomy from the matrix of dependence and slavery that people find themselves in when they do start the unfolding towards truth and harmony. Oligarchic suppression has had imperialistic and fascist clutches globally with its obsession with short-term profits beyond the margins of the Earth's natural resources.

Individuals have begun to question the true motivations of the international oligarchic agenda to control food, medicines and our health and education choices, while more money is perpetually invested in war rather than environmental issues, or making our cities, communities, energy and food resources sustainable. Public transparency is required for anyone who regulates government spending of taxes without public consultation, on military and black projects. Creating more transparency for the public at least regulates, and will eventually dissipate, the severely corrupt system going on within the vaults of closed government departments. We need transparency on so many levels and we need to completely restructure the system, politically, socially and economically. But instead of that, surveillance on civilians is increased and everything is being done to decrease regulations on present governments, elite and corporations, protecting their power interests and giving them further privileges that elevate their status to a place which is above the law.

"*Never forget that no government has wealth of its own to spend. The money has to come from taxation, monetary inflation, or debt expansion that must be paid later. And government's spending choices will always be uneconomic relative to how society would use that wealth. That is to say, the money will be wasted.*"– Llewellyn H. Rockwell, Jr."

Equality can be integrated into new sustainable communities by evolving a non-judgmental way of being and working with one another. Equality builds trust, whereas hierarchical and religious structures create a climate of mistrust, domination and fear, fragmenting and dis-empowering individuals and communities. We can adapt to our changing environment by withdrawing ourselves as 'currency' from the archaic systems of power. We can do this by simply no longer "buying" into this system and making lifestyle and ethical choices to consciously act and live more sustainably and respectfully towards one another and the Earth.

Humanity is evolving faster than the capitalist machine that it has been tricked into serving under, therefore in order to survive economic and environmental changes, we must learn to take responsibility for ourselves, to create new sustainable systems. During the current global "economic collapse", there is an opportunity for us to create a sustainable economy that is within the means of the Earth's natural resources, this would be natural capital which could have the power to enrich previously poor countries and wipe off world debt as well as making people treat nature with more respect as some people unfortunately have to put a financial value on things in order to respect those things. If this is the only way we can get some people to respect Nature, then so be it.

Despite our planet accommodating nearly seven billion people, it is a myth that over-population is the main reason for straining the Earth's natural resources. More than half of the world's population lives on less than a dollar a day - this is the half that the west has turned into slave nations via international trading treaties, commissions and biotechnology companies controlling the world's food, outsourcing production in these conveniently disposable slave nations. There are more than five billion people who live with little access to adequate shelter, clean water, food, education or health care. The remaining western world puts the biggest strain on the planet. Yet, we can switch our economy to one based on natural capital, and wipe off third world debt and new wealth would be instilled in the world's currently poorest nations in the form of the natural capital which they sit on. Energy and agricultural systems would become more sustainable, when we do eventually start to use more exotic alternative energy systems domestically and industrially, we will have more than enough resources for mankind. While governments and their official departments presently mismanage resources via centralised power structures, we will continue to have disparity and poverty.

Looking back at ancient agricultural systems, before resources were controlled by distant powers, we survived very well with localised ecological farming techniques, this is what we can breathe new life into. If every community put local resources and manpower into this, we could still build bridges as a step in the right direction without having to wait for governments to change. If every family had an acre or more of land in which to grow their own food, we would not know poverty. We, the people, have a right to take back management of local natural resources such as water and crops in a sustainable and localised way. Money, greed and centralisation of global power over natural resources is strained and volatile. The present centralisation of power creates the illusion that natural resources are scarce, solely because governments profit from this illusion.

Overpopulation myths are used as one of many veils to perpetuate unethical world debt, trading sanctions and land laws along with other excuses for orchestrated genocides as means to sponsor wars. The problem is 'centralisation' of power and the fiercely guarded secret that humanity sits upon powerful advanced energy technology and chemical-free rain engineering technology, while governments profit from pollution and drought. This advanced technology can provide every single human being with abundant clean water, fertile soil, sustainable food sources and free energy.

While the oligarchic elite vehemently guard control of their central power, it can only result in an accelerating ecological imbalance and human suffering with ecocidal and genocidal consequences, it is logical to say that this ship is sinking when those in charge are only interested in profit and are not acting with any morality or ecological values for Earth or human kind. It is the perfect illustration that financial greed has outgrown itself to the point of destruction - a sure sign that human values need to change.

Unfortunately, people in western society are unlikely to do anything about this unless it starts to affect their quality of life, and as for the oligarchy, it will be a long time before they begin to feel the pinch since they are extremely wealthy and control everything, so they are highly unlikely to make any changes. Those of us who are experiencing the full blow of the current environmental crisis are most likely the poorest and the rural indigenous in developing nations who are paying with their daily lives. The fisherman and farmers are already feeling the effects, indigenous land defenders are immediate targets and victims, they are courageous and continue to stand up against adversity even if it means death, and that while governments are suppressing sustainable technologies that could transform fuel, energy and water into abundant resources.

Capitalism as it is at present, can no longer survive the way in which it is currently driving consumerism and management of global resources and finances. Centralisation of natural resources makes people in poor countries poorer, it allows the Western world to unjustly outsource to produce slaves in slave nations and exploit natural resources in developing countries. These are the unethical products of Capitalism from which we must move away. We must avoid other previous political '*isms*' that have carried destructive elements of fascism, and which do not nurture self-empowerment of the individual and the community. There has to be a balance.

We can transform towns and cities into self-sustaining communities, which will redefine the balance globally and allow indigenous people in poor countries to reclaim their natural resources and land to grow their own food again, to make natural resources publicly-regulated resources, including water, electricity and fuel. Countries such as Africa, Central, South America and India still suffer while privatisation of natural resources such as water, geological natural resources and even the food they grow continue to be managed by giant corporations based in the US and the EU. When we do start living more sustainably in the western world, we give back the freedom to those continents that have been treated as slave nations and allow them to re-establish their own public sustainable natural resources.

Privatisation and 'scarcity' is also something we in the Western cultures have been experiencing due to mismanagement of Nature's capital. Water can be managed as a sustainable resource, we have learned of revolutionary ways to extract abundant water out of air to transform the lives of communities in deserts by using technologies such as Trevor James Constable's rain-engineering technology and other kinds of water-extracting systems. Already tested in many countries such as Malaysia for example, these systems have been government-certified to create rain and successfully clean up pollution. Despite these and other such pioneering methods being vehemently suppressed by governments, the list for sustainable technology possibilities is continuing to expand, thanks to the courageous people who risk their lives to bring such technology into the public eye. These technologies are exciting to implement and experiment with, from 3D printing to Free Energy

"We could build anything we choose to build and fulfil any human need. It is not money that people need; rather, it is free access to the necessities of life. In a resource-based economy, money would be irrelevant." — Jacque Fresco

This old system will not work for much longer, as it has outgrown its ecological and economic niche. After all, the word 'economy' is defined by how communities of people choose to use their environmental resources to meet their chosen living requirements, therefore it is 'us' as a community, who have the power to change the direction of humanity, and not governments.

My hope is, that the information in this book will inspire people to move from our present, unsustainable way of living on Earth, to a way of living for humanity that builds new systems for new ways of being. We have the ability to create change in our local communities, change is a product of communal action and communication. Sustainable living opportunities are choices which we create by how we utilise and engineer water, alternative energy, recycling, food production and soil management. Sustainability also extends to conserving our personal rights as to where we buy our food, how we grow our food, and the availability of herbs and alternative health therapies and products, which it is our right to use in addition to mainstream medicine, so that we can maintain our health in a sustainable way.

These are choices which we have a right to defend. We can do this by looking at the principles of deep ecology which really are not much different to the principles and beliefs of the native indigenous people of the world. The way to go is to give Earth the same rights as a human being; in fact it is our duty as guardians of nature to do this. If a Corporation can become a fictitious 'person' in a court of law, then Nature has far more rights than that of a Corporate entity as it is, in scientific terms, a living organism and a network of ecosystems that sustain life for all creatures. We are beginning to assign Nature economic value for the goods and services which we do not see. Services, such as oxygen production and the pollination services of insects, such as bees and butterflies. Nature is only beginning to be recognised in this way in a court of law, where it can be represented by any non-governmental organisation or individual, therefore it is imperative that Nature be assigned more rights than corporate entities.

In 1972 the Sierra Club won a lawsuit to stop Walt Disney building a Ski resort in the Sierra Wilderness. William Douglas was a key person in the case defence, he stated that –

"*Contemporary public concern for protecting Nature's ecological equilibrium should lead to the conferral of standing upon environmental objects to sue for their own preservation, a ship has a legal personality, a fiction found useful for maritime purposes.... The ordinary corporation is a 'person' for purposes of the adjudicatory processes, whether it represents proprietary, spiritual, aesthetic or charitable causes. So it should be as respects valleys, alpine meadows, rivers, lakes, estuaries, beaches, ridges, groves of trees, swampland or even air that feels the destructive pressures of modern technology and modern life.*"- William Douglas.

There is an international Alliance for the Rights of Nature that has been set up. Every year, they hold a summit where individuals and organisations from all over the world take part and are encouraging politicians and governments to join in the Universal declaration for the rights of Nature. There is now a specialist Earth Law Centre set up in Oakland, California. Their mission statement says "*The Earth Law Centre educates and advocates for laws and policies that recognise and promote the inherent rights of Nature to exist, thrive and evolve. We envision a future where the inherent rights of Nature are respected and implemented globally''*.

There are lawyers such as Polly Higgins, who founded the organisation 'End Ecocide' and Linda Sheehan who is part of the 'Earth Law Centre' who are campaigning to put Environmental Law protection back on the internationally recognised body of laws. The End Ecocide organisation has drawn up a petition that individuals can sign, asking the European and International Union to make ecocide a crime. The last time I checked there were 187,196 signatories and by the time you read this book, the number will have multiplied for a global call named the "Charter of Brussels" which officially requests the establishment of a European and an International Criminal Court of the Environment and Health, to end Ecocide on Earth.

The Charter calls for the recognition of environmental crimes (and crimes against human health), as crimes against Humanity and Peace by the United Nations and is now open for signatures by individuals and organisations and will be handed over to Ban Ki-Moon, UN Secretary-General, the latest during the COP21 Climate Conference in December 2015 in Paris. It is long overdue that Earth should have rights. We need laws to protect Earth from exploitative corporate developments. These are all important steps to progress that will create positive change and progressive laws for the rights of Nature.

We, as humanity, have forgotten the importance and value of communities, which are a gateway for us to move away from global governance to local community commons, so as to be able to disengage from the controlling corporate pressures on Earth's natural resources to self-empowerment and more independence for local communities.

Governments in the UK and the USA have spent the last forty years fragmenting communities by cutting back or withdrawing funds on public education and community projects. Communities do not need to rely on capitalism to thrive; we now have crowd-funding and peer-to-peer funding.

The responsibility lies with each of us to use this time in our lives, without inhibition, to experiment, pioneer and refine solutions that interest us by putting sustainability into action, it can restore that self-esteem which we used to gain from being innovative contributors to our local communities, or a new-era of pioneers for sustainable development. We can work together as a conscious community to implement the best solutions, taking our energy and focus away from dependence on an archaic political system that has destructive values and that has failed to serve humanity. The capitalist machine is a self-serving system sacrificing the planet and humanity, but each of us can transform it into a green capitalism, a new ecological system which could work for the benefit of humanity and a more harmonious relationship with the Earth. We can put our energy into focusing on developing more green technologies and continued refinement to undo what has been done, to renew and rejuvenate the Earth and ourselves. The ultimate message is not only in what is said, but in the way we choose to live our daily lives, so please choose to walk with nature.

The author Carlita Shaw with Shiwiar Chief, Hernan. August, 2012. Photo credit Samuel Remerand. If you would like to contact the author please email

TheSilentEcocide@gmail.com or visit www.thesilentecocide.com

CPSIA information can be obtained at www.ICGtesting.com
Printed in the USA
LVOW04s0044120815

449705LV00024B/692/P

9 781512 365719